KVETCH

KVETCH

T.R. WITOMSKI

INTRODUCTION BY JOHN PRESTON

CELESTIAL ARTS
BERKELEY, CALIFORNIA

Introduction copyright © 1989 by John Preston.

Copyright © 1989 by T.R. Witomski. All rights reserved. No part of this book may be reproduced in any form, except for brief review, without the written permission of the publisher.

CELESTIAL ARTS
P.O. Box 7327
Berkeley, California 94707

Some of this material originally appeared in slightly different form in *The Long Island Connection, Gay Community News,* and *Drummer.*

Cover design by Ken Scott
Text design and composition by Jeff Brandenburg, ImageComp

Library of Congress Cataloging-in-Publication Data

Witomski, T. R., 1953–
     Kvetch/T.R. Witomski; introduction by John Preston.
       p. cm.
     "Some of the material originally appeared in slightly different form in *The Long Island Connection, Gay Community News,* and *Drummer"*—T.p. verso.
     ISBN 0-89087-578-2
     1. Homosexuality—United States.   I. Title
PN4874.W685A25   1989
306.76'6'0973—dc20   89-33655 CIP

First Printing, 1989
0 9 8 7 6 5 4 3 2 1

Manufactured in the United States of America

CONTENTS

Introduction

by John Preston

T.R. Witomski's first magazine article was "*Variations* Visits a Torture Chamber" in 1978. Since that historic moment, I'm not sure if the loudest screams have been heard from his critics or his fans or his many editors. And I'm not *at all* sure which are the inhabitants of that torture chamber.

I am quite convinced that the essay announced T.R. Witomski as one of the most entertaining and insightful writers who ever published in the erotic press. It showed that no subject was too bizarre for him to explore. It proved that no assignment was too outrageous. He put himself on the front lines of the sexual revolution and announced his willingness to scrawl off untold numbers of pages for such journals as *Uncensored Letters* and *Juggs*, to cite only a pair, and to avoid naming any of the more scandalous periodicals whose mastheads were graced with his numerous pseudonyms.

Erotic publishing was Grub Street for many writers in the seventies. There were few places where a beginner could get his or her work (and, when he or she chose, his or her name) into print. The sexual revolution had created a market for writing that seemed limitless. *Mandate*, *Torso*, and the like all proved a perfect match for someone like T.R. There was lucre for confession, there was payment for exposure, there was reward for exhibitionism. T.R. was in heaven.

The chance to write about sex and all its manifestations was probably even more important for those of us who were gay. T.R. was educated in the Roman Catholic church. He spent the first eight years of his schoolboy days in the hands of the Jesuits; the other nine at the mercy of the Dominicans. These were not cultural communities that were eager to help in the development of a public gay identity. Like many others of us, he suffered from that repression of his character and he decided that, unlike excursions into certain theatrical torture chambers, this was not the nice kind of pain and ritual. He wanted something more. Gay liberation gave it to him.

When T.R. came out—when he decided that he was going to be gay and began publicly to acknowledge it—he came out with a vengeance. The decade that followed Stonewall saw a breaking down of barriers, a sharp openness, and an equally pointed awareness that the years of denial, which had been the norm for homosexuals through history, had been dangerous. Gay men of the generation to which T.R. and I belong decided to turn our lives into proof of the assertion. Whatever had been denied was now embraced. Whatever had been censored was now to be published. Whatever had been avoided was now to be explored, and with gusto.

We decided that there was something wrong with ignoring the truths in our lives. There was something just not right about hiding our proclivities, no matter what they were. Before the specter of life-threatening diseases brought a sudden end to it, tens of thousands of gay men in leather jackets were bursting through the barricades of erotic repression and celebrating parts of our lives that had always been hidden.

T.R. was taking notes while it was all going on.

The stretch of periodicals that published T.R.'s writing continued to expand. It was quite astonishing. Even during those times of emancipation, gay writers usually stayed in a pre-allocated niche, seeking comfort in their roles. They were satisfied to conquer the world of erotic journals where T.R. began, for instance. Or else their bylines were found only in the most politically correct publications, where radical lesbian feminists debated the impact of gender on South African economics with drag queens. Still others were happiest in the gay version of straight journalism, writing news stories for the large network of homosexual papers that were springing up from coast to coast.

Not T.R.

He was all over the place, discussing the latest and most aesthetic S&M technique in *Drummer*, writing political analysis in *Gay Community News*, contemplating alcoholism in *The Advocate*. The forces that had unleashed T.R. from his closet had liberated a pen that would not cease writing. The sexual revolution had opened an inkwell that could not be stopped.

By 1980, T.R. had even gotten to that unfamiliar territory where a writer wakes up and realizes, "Oh, my *gawd*. I can make a living at this stuff." But, like many of us, he couldn't do it in New York, where he'd moved after finishing Saint Peter's College in his home state of New Jersey. It's one thing to make a go at writing for a living, another thing to do it while paying Big Apple rents. T.R. wasn't the only one who'd taken enough notes from his life on the Gotham fast-track to last a lifetime. The provinces beckoned. Off he'd go, he decided.

To Orlando.

It makes as much sense as any other decision he'd make in his life. Trust me. I first began to correspond with T.R. when he lived in central Florida. I understood. Sort of. I had moved to Portland, Maine, at the same time, an utter coincidence. We hadn't known each other beforehand. Why Orlando? I finally asked, after I'd gotten to know him a bit.

"Why not Orlando?" was a response I couldn't really challenge from my spot on the rocky coasts. But I did press for an answer. "Look," T.R. told me, "this is an easy life for a writer. Do you know there are grapefruit trees in everyone's backyard? *Grapefruit trees!* The check's late, you go out and pluck a couple. You eat, whether or not the miserable bastards send you the check. What are *you* going to eat? Pine cones? I got grapefruit. I'm happy. Leave me alone."

(One theme T.R. would never let go of was the treatment of writers by publishers. The late check, the check that was perpetually in the mail, the foul-up of assignments and deadlines—all of it made him furious. He didn't sit on that animation, either. He was one of the first and always one of the most ferocious proponents of the National Writers Union. He'd never hesitate to call in the NWU's lawyers when a publisher was messing with him, and he didn't think any other writer should either. "I do a job, I should get a check. What's so strange about that? Why don't they *all* belong to the union?" T.R.'s battles with publishers are the stuff of epics.)

Life in Orlando did put T.R. in touch with the mainstream of gay men. The proudly self-pronounced pornographer took notes on the fantasies of the men who lounged around the pool at the Parliament Hotel, the local gay gathering place, and he fulfilled them. Do you want a coach who'll do you in the lockerroom? T.R. will give it to you in your own story in the next issue of *Hombre Scene*. You've always wanted a motorcyclist in a leather jacket to tie you up? Just read *Honcho* next month; T.R.'s arranged everything. You always wanted to do it with *what?!* Not to worry, T.R. will find a place to publish it, somehow. There's always *Adult Diaper News* or something.

It was an awesome display of sheer talent and complete prolificacy. There were grapefruit in the trees, and there were articles in the print. What more could you want?

Certainly he didn't seem to want respect from the self-appointed guardians of gay literature. As T.R.'s name began to appear in more and more venues, an army of critics rose to challenge him. He discovered that the revolution that had brought about his personal freedom had also brought rules. The problem was, no one had ever told him about those regulations and he'd be damned if he was going to follow them when he hadn't been consulted in the drafting stage.

Who *cared* if a clique of authors were declared the new gay *literati*? He threw boulders at their glass houses. One after another of the darlings of the publishing world were brought down by his pen as he rose to the role of literary critic. "They're wasting more paper on *him?!*" he'd scream. "There are trees dying so that bitch can write another novel?!" There was no justice! T.R. was obsessed.

But then, he'd been obsessed by every topic he wrote about. Men who write guides to torture chambers aren't accidental tourists. This was someone who had a mission in life, and the mission was truth. Probably the highest calling for a writer. Some people wondered about the extent of this man's sanity. Certainly his willingness to become the most outspoken commentator on every aspect of the gay press was seen as self-defeating. (An essay on the quality—or lack thereof—of gay newspapers was published by *Philadelphia Gay News*, just to prove he wasn't prejudiced by attacking *only* gay fiction writers. Anyone was fair game for T.R.) How could anyone who was constantly attacking the very people who could help establish a writer's career ever expect to get anywhere?

The question missed the essential point about T.R. and his craft. The career wasn't the issue. (There were always those grapefruit, or there would always be a new Mafia-supported pornographic publication that could write a check when they were suppose to or some sleazy paperback publisher who just had to have a new tome on god-knows-what kind of kink.) The point wasn't the idea of a socially sanctioned career, the point was the truth of the matter. That was the calling to which T.R. had answered. *What's the truth?* Then tell it, damn it, avoid denying it, get on with it.

Sometimes it did seem that T.R. was going off the deep end with his obsessions. I gingerly asked him recently if he thought he was crazy. "I'm not psychotic," was the answer, "I am neurotic." What does that mean? "Look, if you're psychotic, you don't know where you are. You're so nuts, you haven't a clue. If you're neurotic, you do know where you are but you *do not* like it. I do not like where I am."

Where he is, is a world in which people don't understand that they're nuts. They worry about the wrong things. The idea of liberation is subverted by organizers who don't understand how to schedule a parade; publishers who say inept writers are geniuses; politicians who lie; world leaders who ignore essential civil rights; voters who elect Reagan and Bush to the White House. What is wrong with this picture?

This foolishness must be stopped! That's the message T.R. constantly sends out. *Look at what you're doing!* Oh, and he gave the message anywhere he could. His battles with lesbian feminists and gay/lit/crit mavens in the pages of newspapers from California to Massachusetts to Washington are legend. The gauntlet of a letter to the editor was one that, whenever thrown down, T.R. could not resist. He could not stand to let a challenge go unmet. He would not have it! Not long after T.R. moved back to New York in 1983, this feverish energy finally met a master.

Gerry Robinson had taken on the questionable task of editing a newspaper to challenge *The Native* as New York's gay voice. *The Connection* began circulation on Long Island, then later moved into the vicious Manhattan market. It needed good copy to challenge the competition. It needed new voices. It needed someone who could write. It needed T.R. Witomski.

One of the great difficulties most gay writers face is the lack of space for their ideas. Most publications, newspapers or magazines, work with tight formulas that allow only a few paragraphs for a book review, seven manuscript pages for a major feature article. The limits are oppressing and they don't allow for the development of an idea or a talent.

T.R. had ideas, and he had talent, and, wonders of wonders, *The Connection* had plenty of white space to fill. T.R. was sent out to do battle with all the forces of stupidity he saw on the horizons of his life. Duplicitous politicians, writers with self-inflated egos, gay manias about social status, fixations on stars, opera, old movies—all of those were fair game for the now truly liberated pen of T.R.

Those were wonderful days for gay writing. T.R. was set free, and his targets went crazy. For a period of time, T.R. went wild. And anyone with any intelligence ducked. If they didn't, they got caught by his acidic ink.

Most of the articles in this volume come from that heyday. Reading them is a sad reminder that there aren't many papers left today that have the sweep of *The Connection*. Because so many gay publications are caught up in various political campaigns, overwhelmed by AIDS, or carefully manufactured to fit a predetermined mold, there just aren't many places where a gay writer can come to the top of his form the way T.R. did in *The Connection*. Finances eventually did the paper in, and no one's quite sure about the story of those economics, though a lot a people are still waiting for the check, and I doubt they all have grapefruit trees in their lawns.

The eventual demise of *The Connection* didn't stop T.R. Please, don't let me be misunderstood on that count. Rather, Gerry Robinson and *The Connection* gave T.R. a focus and a chance to polish his style. Certainly, they gave his wonderful wit a chance to expand and find its full force.

T.R. has gone on. Of course he has. After *The Connection* folded, someone in a bar challenged T.R. to publish in the home of the *literati* he'd so often offended. "Darling, of course I can." T.R. went to his typewriter and spun off an article that duly appeared in *The Native* within the next few weeks. "Just to show them I can do it," he announced to me.

Wit and observation, and above all truth, have been the hallmarks of T.R. Witomski's contribution to gay writing. For more than a decade he's been telling the facts as he saw them, not as someone who was willing to accept them as they were. "I know where I am *and I do not like it*" remains his creed. He is the perfect kvetch.

The kvetch in us all isn't just a nay-sayer, after all, the kvetch in us all is a truth-sayer. *I don't like it!* It's one of the statements that always must be spoken before things can change. It's a call to arms, a speaking of the word. There's a bit of the holy man in all of this, perhaps the antic shaman who's so revered in many traditional cultures, perhaps even remnants of the speaker of the gospel in T.R.'s Roman catholic background. Whatever it is, T.R. embodies it.

This collection of essays is a great chance for many new readers to discover one of the voices of authenticity that has been speaking for the gay everyman.

—John Preston
Portland, Maine
August 1989

Genesis

What I thought I'd do here is describe, more in sorrow than in anger, how this book came to be written . . .

It was a dark and stormy night shortly after the Fall of Constantinople, and I was, as continues to be my habit to this very day, amusing myself in a leather bar where I chanced to make what was considered by a well hung stud with an amazingly low IQ to be a vaguely amusing remark about an ersatz policeman with a bone through his nose.

"You should," the stud (10½", 36 on the Stanford-Binet) said, "write a book."

Though I might have preferred that the stud have said, "You should ready your face for me to sit upon," I was prepared at that point to accept any suggestion from such a specimen. God alone knows what turns some people on.

So I wrote a really funny little book devoted to elucidating the witty adventures of a madcap writer at the baths and sex bars of Constantinople and New York and San Francisco and Los Angeles and Key West and Provincetown and Cleveland and Peoria and Sydney and Oslo and Manila and Havana and Machu Picchu and Rome and Nome and Chillicothe. So impressive was this tome that a well known editor at a very prestigious publishing house used the manuscript for three years as a clever doorstop and receptacle for empty butyl nitrate bottles at his summer home in Fire Island Pines before declining to publish it "because it needs an editor."

By this time a rather ugly, painful, horrible, lingering, annoying, lethal—did I mention lingering?—disease—you know the one—had made its debut, and a goodly number of the folks who had shared the witty adventures of a madcap writer at the baths and sex bars of Constantinople and New York and San Francisco and so on and so on and so on (and who might be counted on to buy a book about same) had passed on to The Heavenly Eagle and The Club Baths Elysian Fields.

Not the best of decades for the vaguely amusing. You couldn't joke about you-know-what, though personally I found the fact that gay bar chit chat now resembled the talk at an editorial meeting of the *Medical Alert Digest* a laugh riot. A vaguely amusing cocksucker in the midst of the greatest gay trauma since the demise of Judy Garland was not exactly in wild publishing demand so you can imagine my delighted surprise when I saw in the want ads of *The New York Times*:

VAGUELY AMUSING COCKSUCKER. For Homosexual [The *Times* at that time refused to print "gay" unless it meant "happy" and sometimes not even then] newspaper. Unbelievable pay. Contact Gerry Robinson at The Long Island Connection at (516) XXX-XXXX.

(I swear on a gross of condoms that while my memory of the exact wording of the ad may be slightly inexact, my recall of its basic sense is right on the money, though money, as in any enterprise that involves homosexuals and newspapers, had nothing to do with it.)

Fate or what? What, it turned out. However, the *Times* doesn't lie: The pay was truly unfuckinbelievable. But Gerry Robinson was an editor with more than half a brain and, rumor had it, a very big dick as well. Only those in the vaguely amusing cocksucker biz will understand the rarity and enormity of Gerry's accomplishments. The ideas for most of the vaguely amusing essays here originated in his more than half a brain. (Another miracle: It's well known that most editors of—what is that *Writer's Market* phrase?—"homosexually oriented journalism/fiction," edit with their dicks, which just goes to show you that gay publications aren't dependent on natural ability. You, too, could get a job editing *Safe Fisting Quarterly*.)

You see, I was content to hang around leather bars making vaguely amusing pronouncements until Gerry said, "Get out of The Spike, queen!"

"But where can I go?" Sounds pitiful, doesn't it? I envisioned a local TV reporter getting into semi-butch drag to do a five-part series during sweeps weeks on "Leatherbarless in America."

"Go to . . . go to Bloomingdale's. Go to the fuckin' Metropolitan Opera. Go seduce a straight man; you won't find one here. Go slum with the A-gays. Go to the goddamned movies, for Kim Novak's sake!"

Obedient to a fault, I followed Gerry's advice, and the results are what you'll be reading.

Due to the vagaries of gay newspapers (printers with dyslexia, publishers with 5K a day cocaine habits, distributors who demand two-hour work weeks and all the pasta and cement they need), Gerry is no longer encouraging vaguely amusing cocksuckers to be vaguely amusing in print.

"Do you realize that there are jobs out there that give you checks that don't bounce every week?"

I had no idea.

So I went back to those leather bars until Paul Reed, half-brainy, hung editor of the nice book you're holding in your nice hands, intervened to say, "Excuse me for interrupting your leather barring, but might some of those vaguely amusing essays of yours make a book?"

Fate or what?

What.

Now I'm wondering if Oxford University Press would care for a tome called *The Renaissance of the Vaguely Amusing Cocksucker in What Passes for Literature These Days*. Introduction by John Preston.

In my somewhat less than glory days, I wrote some 300 porn novels, but this book is my first "real book" (*Enema Nurses in Bondage* and *She-Male Diaper Sluts* were, if nothing else, unreal and never made much of an impression at the ABA Convention) and I'd like to dedicate it to the memory of Roy Wood, Tom Held, and Joe Smenyak—three of the many thousands.

—T.R. Witomski
Toms River, New Jersey

1

IT'S A WONDERFUL GAY LIFE

All this talk about homosexuality having a biological basis has certainly created an uproar here in gay press land. Publishers and editors of gay periodicals, by nature whiners, have been given something new to whine about: "But if people can go have shots—or something—to make them straight and if prenatal fags can be cured, who's gonna be around to buy this publication?" But the more important question is: what's gonna happen to the publishers and editors of gay periodicals, who simply are unable to get jobs in the real world, should the universe turn straight? (Idea for a follow-up: can gay *publications* be cured? There's really no need for them. Every fag already knows what every other fag is doing. The publications exist only to tell us who got caught.)

No fear. The publisher of *The Advocate* will never have to go to work as a receptionist in the corporate offices of Kentucky Fried Chicken. As Einstein wrote, $f(x)>qc$ (cubed). This equation, better known as the universal conservation of faggotry, proves that homosexuals are essential to the way the cosmos works. Though the full complexities of this law are understood only by a few top scientists and hairdressers, laypeople can see its indisputable veracity in the famous statement of Nancy Reagan's: "If you get rid of all the cocksuckers, who will do the windows at Bloomingdale's?"

Who indeed? Not even the most savage homophobe would want to look at a window display done by a heterosexual. Oh *Please*! And who would submit to a scissors-wielding straight screeching, "Let's try something *really* kicky with your hair"? Not *moi*. There *are* limits, darling. Even to my submission.

World Without Fags

A world without fags would not be a very pleasant place. Sure, you'd still get up in the morning and the TV news shows would still be on. But without those adorable and oh-so-clever little gay make-up people, Jane Pauley and Bryant Gumbel would look like Lillian Hellman and W.H. Auden, not exactly the sight one wants to see in the a.m. (A joke at the expense of the dead! Such poor taste! What the fuck do you expect at these prices? Subtlety is extra.)

The workplace would not be any better. The bright-eyed and cheery office queen would not be at his post by the water cooler to tell you just what Marsha did with Mr. Baumgarten last night in the stockroom. Faggots invent gossip, and if we go, we are taking all the gossip with us.

And don't think that after work you'll be able to go to your favorite restaurant for dinner. Well, you could *go* but don't expect any service. A little known law makes it illegal for heterosexual men to be waiters.

Forget about the theatre, too. Take all the faggot actors, singers, dancers, directors, costume designers, set directors and all-purpose show queens out of the theatre and you'll be left with *A Chorus Line* sans book, sans music, sans clothes, sans performers, sans *everything*. We are talking serious minimalism here. Opera won't fare much better. Marilyn Horne ain't gonna show up to perform for the six people who'd be left in the Met audience after the fags leave.

Have I mentioned dancing yet? There will be none of that in the brave new straight world. Faggots have a patent on dance steps. The last heterosexual who invented a new dance was Friar Lindihop in 1246. (And, to tell the truth—don't I always?—we're not too sure about the good friar.)

But you'll probably not really notice the absence of dancing since there'll be no place left to go dancing anyway. It takes *tons* of gays to transform all those warehouses, old movie houses, and churches into dance Meccas. Heterosexuals are simply unable to say, "Look, Mary—a slaughterhouse! Let's turn it into a disco."

The Demise of Chic

I also have bad news about gentrification. You know how chic it is to go to the East Village on Saturdays and see faggots painting, faggots planting, faggots plastering, faggots announcing "This wall has *got* to go." (And since no homos means no dykes, too—ya always get the good with the bad—they'll be no one around to devalue good neighborhoods, causing chaos in the real estate business.) In a world without gays, deteriorating neighborhoods will stay that way.

The good neighborhoods are also dependent on gays. Just look at all those lovely gay cleaning services. If you need your $50,000 Queen Anne table dusted, you want the person who's doing the dusting to envy what he's dusting. And all those cute little shops selling useless doodads, the ones that give a neighborhood "character" will be a thing of the past should hets take over. Heterosexuals sell furniture; gays sell living center arrangements to die for. Who wants mere furniture in a two million dollar co-op? Just think: without homosexuals, Jackie O will be reduced to living in squalor since there will be no one to advise her on wallpaper.

And don't forget—Christ, this essay is supposed to go for 1500 words and I haven't a clue what to do for the rest of it. Don't blame me; it wasn't my idea to write this. Wouldn't you rather read about what Gerard Robinson was doing at The Anvil at 6 a.m. two days before deadline? *Not editing*—that's for damn sure. Or I could reveal a lot of scandalous gossip about writers, the sort of thing John Preston always makes me swear on Grandma's grave never to reveal. How about a few Andrea Dworkin jokes? (What's the difference between Andrea Dworkin and a rampaging elephant? The overalls.) Maybe my recipe for pecan cookies?

Answered Prayers

Meanwhile, back in the all-straight world, TV ministers with no one to bleach and tease their hair and do make-up will be upset. Their prayers have been answered. No one is sucking cock anymore who's any good at it. The good reverends have nothing to rave about, the lack of available good head being an unacceptable subject for prime-time homilies. You remember the good old days. Gather round the television and hear Rev. Jerry Foulmouth say, "Yes, brothers and sisters in Jesus, San Francisco is just like Sodom, only with cable cars. Look at this 8x10 color glossy of—dare I expose you to a glimpse of Hell? I asked Jesus whether I should exhibit this vile picture to Christian men and women, and Jesus said, 'Oh, why not?' Send your children out of the room while you look at this photograph of Sister Boom Boom—and worse. Luckily, Jesus has told me how to solve the problem of homosexuality. For a love offering of $24.95—checks payable to cash—Jesus will tell you, too."

It was so inspiring. And it worked too well, because in a world without homosexuals, the Moral Majority types will be unable to amuse the electronic congregation. Sermons will become boring. And boredom will translate into empty bank accounts for fundamentalist preachers. Though drinking, gambling, and fornication will still be around, nothing can take the place of homosexuality.

Absence of faggots will create great consternation out there where chiggers burrow and Jesus saves. The ministers will realize that a desperate problem demands a final solution. So they will put pressure on the federal government to turn ten percent of the heterosexual population into homosexuals by giving them—shots or something. In short order, the landscapes will once again be dotted with homosexuals of every hue. And everyone will be able to get a decent haircut.

T.R. Witomski's Recipe for Pecan Cookies

1½ cups butter or margarine, softened
1 cup firmly packed light brown sugar
2 teaspoons granulated sugar
2½ cups all-purpose flour
2 cups chopped pecans
2 teaspoons buttermilk or plain yogurt
½ teaspoon baking soda
½ teaspoon ginger
½ teaspoon cinnamon
¼ teaspoon nutmeg

Preheat oven to 375 degrees F. Grease two very large cookie sheets. In large mixing bowl cream butter or margarine and sugars until light and fluffy. Add remaining ingredients and mix well. Drop rounded teaspoonfuls onto cookie sheets. Bake ten minutes. Cool on wire racks. Makes about 7 dozen, about 60 calories each.

(The above recipe has *not* been warranted. You have been warned.—Ed.)

2

101 THINGS YOU CAN DO WITH A STRAIGHT MAN

1. Go bowling.
2. Play poker.
3. Discuss the girls. (He will talk about the ones he wants to fuck, and you can talk about your friends.)
4. Fight about Billy Martin's last—or next management of the Yankees.
5. Jog.
6. Curse your job.
7. Go to Atlantic City. (No, Mary, *not* to cruise the beach; straight men don't know that there *is* a beach in Atlantic City.)
8. Have a few drinks.
9. Take in a wrestling match. (Refrain from *those* comments; straight men do not understand "I wish he would sit on my face.")
10. Mow the lawn.
11. Fix the car.
12. Paint the house (in a suitably butch color).
13. Fix the toaster.
14. Have a barbecue; remember that the straight man gets to wear the apron.
15. Piss against a wall together.
16. Barf.
17. Go to see *Rambo* XLIV.
18. Take turns reading aloud from *Soldier of Fortune* magazine, which is to straight men what *Drummer* is to you.

19. Go fishing.
20. Suggest that he sit down and write a story about what went on in his high school locker room; mail the story to Boyd McDonald.
21. Explain "write."
22. Explain "what went on."
23. Explain "Boyd McDonald."
24. Forget 20.
25. Drink some more.
26. Pass the poppers. (Yes, darling, *you* as a health conscious fag are eschewing poppers these days, having already inhaled enough of the stuff to turn on everyone in Indiana; most straight men don't know poppers from pap smears.)
27. Offer to bake him a quiche.
28. Inform him where he can get a decent haircut.
29. Avoid looking at the dirt under his fingernails.
30. Prove that you know all about heterosexuality by re-counting the plot of *Tosca*.
31. Sexually enlighten him. Straight men do not know that their tits are erogenous zones. So tell him. *Tell* him.
32. Once you've done tits, move on to the prostate gland.
33. Thanks to the health crisis, you too can now play a game long popular among straight men: "I'll show you the condom I have in my wallet if you show me the condom you have in your wallet."
34. Order another round.
35. Give him some pointers on his tennis game. In the interest of decorum, refrain from mentioning his limp wrist.
36. Educate him about cleanliness: "What do you mean you don't douche before a big date?"
37. Go see *Rambo* CXIV.
38. Fight about Davey Johnson's management of the Mets.
39. Say vile things about George Steinbrenner.
40. Offer a cultural exchange: you'll explain ballet to him if he'll explain football to you.
41. Criticize the way he walks.

42. Make him envious; recount tales of the ten best blow jobs you've ever gotten. (Don't recount tales of the ten best blow jobs you've ever *given*. Straight men are obsessed with getting their cocks sucked, but the idea of sucking a cock upsets them.)

43. All gay men know whether or not they have a big dick, but straight men are terribly uncertain about the size of their cocks. Offer to make an honest appraisal of his equipment.

44. Offer a few kind suggestions on how to improve his wardrobe: "Well, if you think it's masculine to wear a little pansy animal on your shirt, go ahead. I just think it's a little . . . well, you know. . . ."

45. Watch *Tour of Duty.*

46. Puke.

47. Get serious: critique the acting of Tanya Roberts.

48. Smoke some dope. Amuse yourself counting how many times he says "Hey, wow, I'm really stoned, man."

49. Talk about what went on at the baths. Trust me—straight men are absolutely fascinated about the tubs: "Hey, wow, they should have had places like that for us, man."

50. Ask him if you can do him for trade.

51. Explain "do."

52. Explain "trade."

53. If he says yes, announce you were just kidding. Watch him turn lovely shades of crimson.

54. Go to see *Rambo* DXLII. Straight men cannot get enough of Sylvester Stallone's muscles.

55. Encourage him to describe how he'd "cure" Martina Navratilova; picture what would happen to him if he actually tried—"Martina aims the tennis ball to the left testicle in a powerful, savage shot." Grin widely.

56. Visit a liquor store.

57. Admit you've always wanted to own a pick-up truck.

58. Poke fun at the way his jeans fit.

59. Regale him with Mineshaft stories; he will think you're joking.

60. Take him to The Spike.

61. Smoke some more dope. Pretend you're deaf when he starts with, "Hey, wow, I'm so fuckin' horny, I could fuck a pig, man."

62. Let him indulge in his favorite intellectual pursuit. "What kind of beer is the best?"

63. Indulge yourself in your favorite intellectual pursuit: "Do you know that _____ is gay?"

64. Chide him lovingly, "You sure do talk funny."

65. Depress him: "Due to my worry about AIDS, I'm now only having sex regularly with my seventy-two closest fuck buddies. It was so difficult to say no the other 1,231, but I *had* to do it."

66. Listen to him bitch about his divorce. Offer sympathy: "That's just what happened between me and Marvin. And between me and Edwin. And between me and Anatol. And between me and. . . ."

67. A viewing of *Rambo* MDCLVIII. This time bring up the films' homoeroticism.

68. Explain "homoeroticism."

69. Watch him turn lovely shades of green.

70. Oh, go ahead, tell him the answer to the question he's most concerned about: "Do black guys have bigger dicks than white guys?"

71. *More* drinks.

72. Shake him up: list all your gay friends who used to be straight.

73. *Really* shake him up: declare that *you* used to be straight.

74. Make him panic: have him swear to call you *at once* should he find himself "turning" gay.

75. More drinks.

76. Drive him mad by opining, "Isn't it funny that so many straight guys become gay, but except for a few of those silly girls at Aesthetic Realism, almost no one gay becomes straight?"

77. Call Anheuser-Busch; request an emergency delivery.

78. Let him in on a few of the newest dance steps.

79. Remark on anything he says/does, "Oh, are straight men

saying/doing *that* these days?" Watch the other hets move a tasteful distance away from the sexual suspect.

80. Clean out the garage.
81. Soothe his fears: "Just because you once in a while let a gay man suck you off doesn't mean that you are in the least bit queer." Do not giggle while saying this.
82. "Bridge anyone? . . . It's a card game. . . . No, not exactly like poker. More like . . . never mind."
83. Time for another joint. Note: for some unaccountable reason, straight men do not think it the least bit gay to shotgun a joint with another man.
84. Agree that Yogi Berra got shafted.
85. Slander your boss.
86. Pump iron. Straight men love to get all hot and sweaty with other men. Don't ask me why.
87. Be ruthlessly hypercritical about your last trick.
88. Explain "trick."
89. Listen to him explain, "Hey, wow, that sounds just like the chick I balled last year, man."
90. Ask to have "chick" explained.
91. Casually allude to a sexual use for the fist; experience heterosexual bafflement reaching a new height—or depth.
92. Suggest a shopping spree.
93. Punish him by reading out loud from the collected works of Felice Picano.
94. Belch.
95. Tell him that you find it curious that he extends his pinky when he drinks.
96. Offer to take him cruising. Explain that you do not have sailboats in mind.
97. Investigate the possibility of getting a Budweiser pipeline installed in your residence.
98. Satisfy his morbid curiosity by telling him what anal sex feels like.
99. Satisfy your morbid curiosity by asking just why he wants to know this.
100. Lie: "Lots of straight men get fucked in the ass once. It doesn't mean they're queer."

101. Solicit contributions for my new essay, "101 Things You Can Do With a Gay Man."

Special Thanks to Perry Brass and Howard Wuelfing for research assistance.

3

NEVER FORGIVE, NEVER FORGET
Ex-Lovers, Like Diamonds, Are Forever

Everyone complains about ex-lovers, but nobody does anything about them. Though I am unsure as to what exactly a lover is (the common definition that a lover is "a person you have a deep emotional commitment to" describes my computer repairman; even defining a lover a "a person you have a deep emotional commitment to and whom you also fuck on occasion" also describes my computer repairman), I *am* clear about what an ex-lover is. An ex-lover is "a very nice guy who's unfortunately lousy in bed," "a hunky stud who unfortunately will fuck anybody," "a sweet man who's unfortunately a terrible lush," "a great person who unfortunately has no sense of financial responsibility," "a very intelligent number who's unfortunately overly involved with his career," "a great lay who unfortunately is still hung up on his first lover," and "a very beautiful human being who unfortunately is still a Mama's boy." Ex-lovers are, therefore—to a man—unfortunate.

And numerous. While lovers are as rare as lesbians with a sense of humor, ex-lovers are like aphids—they multiply so fast you can't ever get rid of them entirely, no matter how hard you try. How true this is may be seen by going to The Spike with my friend Morris. Morris, you see, is desperate to find a lover. (He is under the illusion that a lover will help him overcome his terrible loneliness, fill up the void of his existence, love him *as a person,* fuck him senseless regularly, pay the rent, and fix his computer, a belief Morris holds to even though I have told him on many occasions that what he really needs is to be severely disciplined.) But on nights at The Spike, all Morris finds are ex-lovers: "There's Jack, my third ex-lover, who is talking to— can it be?—Carmine, my nineteenth ex-lover, and over there is. . . ." At a very conservative estimate, ex-lovers outnumber lovers two hundred to one.

Waiting For Ex-Loverhood

Basically a lover is a person who's just sort of hanging around waiting to become an ex-lover, like a caterpillar waits around to become a moth. The cocoon stage for a lover, which can last anywhere from six minutes to sixteen years, begins the first time it is said of him to a handsome stranger in a bar, "Well, he's not *really* my lover anymore" and ends with a horrible fight over custody of *Born to Raise Hell* and the Diana Ross records.

Sooner or later, everyone turns into an ex-lover. You can even tell when someone is just seconds away from ex-loverhood because that's when he says, "Reginald and I will be lovers forever."

Once you are a certified ex-lover (and some ex-lovers have such a difficulty accepting their new status that they do need to spend time in a rest home), you are one for life. A lot of people think that love is forever and that ex-love is fleeting. It's really exactly the opposite. So many people make this error that it makes me lose my patience. Yes, Bruce and Bob may be lovers today and, as such, merrily boring themselves to tears shopping for dishes at Bloomie's and brunching away in fern-infested Soho restaurants, but not only are they moving rapidly into ex-loverdom, but both are probably already ex-lovers of a few dozen folks. Clearly, then, ex-lovers are more popular than lovers: you can't have too many of them or be one to too many people. The proof of this is simple: show up at a party with more than one current lover and you face disaster; show up with a bunch of ex-lovers (or be one of those ex-lovers) and it's partying as usual. If your lover makes an ass of himself, you'll feel mortified; if your ex-lover makes an ass out of himself—well, *now* everybody knows what ended your relationship with him.

Unity in Divestiture

Ex-lovers unify the homosexual community, making us all one big gay family. Take Bruce and Bob (and maybe you should, they are brunching too much these days and getting fat, fat, fat). Bruce has seven ex-lovers (whom, for simplicity's sake, I'll call A through G, inclusive) and Bob—who was quite randy during his forty-two-year long youth—has sixteen ex-lovers (G through V, inclusive). Now, in addition to Bob's six "sisters" and Bruce's twelve "sisters," with all their current and ex-lovers, these people constitute one gay nuclear family. But wait, there's also the extended family: Bruce's ex-lover A is also related through direct ex-loverhood to G, N, T and W, X, Y and Z, while Bruce's ex-lover B is also the ex-lover of G, T, Y, A2, B2 and C21, and Bruce's ex-lover C is also the ex of G (who's been a *very* busy boy), Z, B2, D2, E2, and . . . but you get my point. Happy families are all alike, unhappy families are unhappy in their own ways, but there is only one gay extended family and we're all in it. Talk about The Family of Man! (If you'd like to find out exactly where *you* fit into the gay family tree, buy my book *Fruits: One Faggot's Search For His Gay Identity*, in which I trace everybody's gay ancestry all the way back to the famous tribe of Neanderthal Gays who once roamed around what is today Warsaw.)

With all these ex-lovers running around, I find it a grave publishing sin that no one has ever written a guide for ex-lovers. If I see one more book or article on "The Gay Couple," I shall surely barf. (I just heard the computers of all the writers in the universe who are doing their own miserable versions of "The Joys of Lovers and Ennui" stop—thanks, guys.) What we need is a study of "The Gay Un-Couple."

One of the reasons ex-lovers are so wonderful and in such demand is that you can pretty much treat them as you please. One is, more or less, expected to act civilized toward a current lover—until you decide that he'd be better suited for the role of an ex-lover. But once the lover has actually metamorphosed into an ex-lover, you finally can be honest in your feelings about him. Let us look at my own ex-love life for some most illuminating illustrations.

Yes, I Remember Them Well

I love to hate Bill. I lived with the son-of-a-bitch for three years, during which time he subjected me to all sorts of humiliations and abominable treatment, some of which I disliked. But my reason for bringing up this sick queen here is not to cast aspersions on him (though his ass *was* unshapely), but to point out that, now that he is an ex-lover, I can sit around and amuse myself despising him. Spending twenty minutes a day actively vilifying an ex-lover is good for your skin and your mental health.

But hating ex-lovers is just one of the things you can do with them. Ex-lovers can also be ignored, as I ignore John H., who used to give me syphilis periodically even though I used to tell him constantly that I'd much prefer being taken out to dinner. Ex-lovers can be recalled fondly, as I fondly recall Chris L., with whom I first went to Provincetown. (Nostalgia compels me to remember only the beauty of that summer and not the fact that Chris was such a tramp that he made Erica Kane seem virginal.) *Parts* of ex-lovers can be fondly recalled, as I recall Fred L.'s cock; it wasn't his fault that there was a vast uncharted wasteland where his mind should have been. Ex-lovers can be whined to, as I whine to Jim C.; he has to pay me back for all those times he whined to me. Ex-lovers can be thanked for their contributions to your education, as I thank Jose G. for teaching me to say, "Stop that right now or I'll murder you slowly and painfully" in Spanish. Ex-lovers can even be forgotten, as I've forgotten. . . .

"The one thing you must *never* do is have sex with an ex-lover. Class, what is the one thing you must *never* do with an ex-lover?"

"Very good, class, that is correct: the one thing you must *never* do is have sex with an ex-lover. Yes, Gerard, you have your hand up; what is it?"

A Socratic Dialogue

"Why should you *never* have sex with an ex-lover?"

"I'm glad you asked me that question, Gerard. Let us use the Socratic Method to come up with an answer. Now, Gerard, before your ex-lover was your ex-lover, what was he?"

"My lover."

"And when he was your lover, wasn't he terribly annoying?"

"Yes, very. Why one time he—"

"In a Socratic dialogue, Gerard, we logically pursue a line of reasoning. There are no time-outs for kvetching. Is that clear?"

"Yes."

"Now, before your ex-lover was your lover, what was he?"

"My boyfriend."

"And before your ex-lover was your boyfriend, what was he?"

"My trick."

"And before your ex-lover was your trick, what was he?"

"A hot-looking guy at a bar."

"Exactly. When your ex-lover was a hot-looking guy at a bar, what did you think of him?"

"I wanted to fuck him for six hours."

"And did you?"

"Yes."

"How was it?"

"Great."

"Exactly. So would you say that a hot-looking guy at a bar became a great trick?"

"Yes."

"What did you think of this great trick?"

"I wanted to fuck him again."

"And did you?"

"Yes."

"Several times?"

"Yes."

"How was it?"

"Fair."

"Exactly. So would you say that a great trick became a fair boyfriend?"

"Yes."

"What did you think of the fair boyfriend?"

"It sounds silly, but I wanted to move in with him."

"Not silly at all. Did he know how to fix computers?"

"Yes."

"Exactly. And did you move in with him?"

"Yes."

"And how was it?"

"Living hell."

"Exactly. So would you say that a fair boyfriend became a lover who made your life a living hell?"

"Yes."

"So you became ex-lovers?"

"Yes."

"Are you both happy being ex-lovers?"

"Yes."

"Now the last time you saw this particular ex-lover, what did you think of him?"

"This might sound strange, but while I *knew* he was my ex-lover, I *thought* he looked like a hot-looking guy at a bar whom I wanted to fuck for six hours."

"Gerard, you have answered your own original question. Fuck an ex-lover and this whole stupid business starts all over again. Are there any more questions about ex-lovers? No? Class dismissed."

4

CRACKING UP:
HOW TO DO
IT RIGHT

I'm always in a state of mild neurosis, but at least once a day the craziness peaks and I can't decide whether it's time to re-establish a close relationship with my former shrink or to declare that cocktail hour has begun. Today's outburst of "I can't stand it anymore" was triggered when I opened the *Philadelphia Gay News* and read that managing editor Stanley Ward was so impressed by some of my recent remarks on the holy subject of pornography that he suggested I "Bury the bitch that weights your wit and the cur that burdens your brain. Children shouldn't play with dead things." I don't know what that means but I don't like the sound of it.

If sanity is a rock, these daily attacks are hammer blows to it. For the record, I have been institutionalized in the past, but only once and briefly. And that was simply the result of a silly mix-up in dosage calculations. When I escaped, I *immediately* changed pharmacies.

Though many people will find this difficult to believe, I already suffer from at least seven major personality defects, as the following excerpts from my journal will attest to. All people who know that they will one day become intimately acquainted with "very restful" surroundings, sinister nurses all doing Louise Fletcher impersonations, Haldol and Sinequan *for days*, and shock therapy, keep journals. As we go totally bonkers, we are thinking of best-sellerdom, movie rights and a TV spinoff—B*A*N*A*N*A*S—starring Alan Alda, Woody Allen, and Joan Collins as ourself. After all, we journal-keeping sickos may be rapidly journeying into irreversible psychosis, but remember: we are *crazy*, we are not *stupid*.

Passages From the Diary of a (Would-Be) Madperson

With brief diagnostic comments from a learned psychiatrist, Dr. G. Stambolian:

❖ *Monday*: A hangover suitable for framing. The landscape people come to do God-only-knows-what with the lawn: four lovely boys (or are they?) with huge, loud machines. Meanwhile, the power company or people disguised to look like they work for New Jersey Power and Light decide to rip up the street. Three strident editors call before 10:00 a.m. How did they all know I had a hangover? Suspect CIA involvement. (*Patient exhibits acute paranoia.*)

❖ *Tuesday*: The present object of my affections (soon to become a former object of my affections) cancels our date tonight because he has to clean his apartment or walk his dog or wash his hair. Tomorrow he's drying his hair—"It's a big job, ya know." (*Murderous urges.*)

❖ *Wednesday*: A humorous essay of mine is rejected because "It's too funny." (*Career anxiety.*)

❖ *Thursday*: A zit appears on my body. Now I *know* I have AIDS. (*AIDSphobia.*)

❖ *Friday*: Mumsy invites me to dinner. Says "Bring your nice self; leave the bitch home." (*Possible split personality.*)

❖ *Saturday*: A peaceful idyll in Atlantic City turns ugly when it becomes apparent that all the blackjack dealers have it in for me. How else to explain losing more than a dozen times while standing on twenty? (*Persecution mania.*)

❖ *Sunday*: I begin to think I am Oliver Twist. I say to an editor, "Please, Sir, I want some more money," and he screams, "Money?!? You want money!?!" Clutching my ragged clothes around me, I sing "Money, Glorious Money." (*Hallucinations—most probably indicative of schizophrenia brought on by consuming too many mind-altering chemicals in the 1960s.*)

Don't suggest therapy. And don't suggest Ann Landers, either. I did consult Ann Landers and, without skipping a beat, she replied, "You and everyone you have ever known need to get counseling immediately." I can't vouch for everyone I have ever known, but if all the therapists that I have consulted in my life were laid end to end, they could act as a human chain to ferry my copy from here to Berkeley, California and ferry back excuses instead of money from Berkeley to here. Obviously, I don't have much faith in mental health professionals, since they allow me to run around unsupervised. I realize I have to do something about my numerous psychic afflictions. But what all those people and editors who tell me "For God's sake, T.R., I've begged you to get some therapy," don't realize is that I *have* gotten therapy, tons of it, and that, according to the therapeutic community, *this* is cured. It's a frightening thought to have to confront the idea that, compared to what I used to be, I am better now. Really.

Gays and Madness

Where does being gay fit into all of this? It doesn't. As much as we may protest to the contrary, gay people aren't any crazier than anyone else. Insanity is an equal opportunity employer; it discriminates not on the basis of race, creed, color, national origin or sexual orientation. Even the great gay loons—Andrea Dworkin, Chuck Ortleb—to name but two—wouldn't be any less off-the-wall if they were possessed of a different sexual appetite.

However, gay people do have a few neurotic behaviors that aren't often found in individuals of the heterosexual persuasion. Straights aren't likely to spend an inordinate amount of time agonizing over which group to march with in the Gay Pride Parade. You rarely hear a straight person sighing deeply and orating, "I don't know *what* to do. It's driving me nuts. I want to march with the Lesbian Sex Mafia, but if I do that the Dykes Against Smut will picket my house because they'll figure I am harboring a copy of *Macho Sluts* in the torture chamber, and if I don't march with Dykes & Tykes, my lover and her fourteen children will beat me up and next year I'll have to march with the Battered Lesbians for Jesus. What will I do? What will I do?" Also, straights tend not to get unduly frantic if they miss reading an issue of *Dungeonmaster*.

Funny, but writing about crackin' up is a lot like writing about ex-lovers. Bouts with insanity and bouts with ex-lovers are perhaps the only two types of experiences that all gays have in common. (And for those of you who are claiming that you are candidates for becoming this year's Mental Health Poster Child, may I gently remind you of those massive hissy fits you throw whenever you discover that, after hieing yourself to Bloomingdale's at the speed of light, those absolutely adorable shoes you *must* have are not available in your size? By no stretch of the imagination may such behavior be considered a shining example of sanity in a world gone mad.) In fact, the parallels between ex-lovers and insanity are striking. Ex-lovers, particularly those who telephone drunkenly at 4 a.m. to discuss their "true feelings," are a chief cause of insanity, and insanity—as manifested by such quirks as a morbid fascination with the films of Maria Montez, or thinking that lip-synching drag queens are a form of entertainment—tends to cause lovers to rush themselves into ex-hood. A study of "Which Came First—the Ex-Lover or the Insanity?" might prove illuminating, though I imagine the answer would be a tie. No doubt about it: ex-lovers and madness are inextricably linked. Just how true this is may be seen in the popular gay pastime: Trying To Get Your Ex-Lover To Pay For Your Therapy. After all, Bruce/Stephanie caused your nuttiness in the first place; you were a paragon of mental wellness before he/she introduced you to booze and/or drugs and/or gambling and/or SM and/or the Pines and/or opera and/or Mars and/or writing for the gay press and/or threesomes and/or interior decoration and/or the National Gay Task Force and/or watching *Dynasty* re-runs and/or reading the novels of Gordon Merrick or Sarah Aldridge.

Doing It Right

Since sooner or later everyone cracks up, you might as well learn how to do it right:

❖ Recognize at once that there is a difference between sincere cracking up and merely whining. An example of the latter: "I have no money, my lover won't put out, and I'm gonna get fired." An example of the former: "I have no money, my lover won't put out, and I'm gonna get fired—and don't think I don't know who's responsible."

❖ True crack-ups must be as public as possible. Sitting home going quietly nuts won't entertain your friends. You must tell people that you're "losing it—and fast" and periodically demonstrate your looniness by performing in an eccentric manner where it can be observed. "Did you see what Harold did at The Spike last night? That boy is definitely one brick shy of a load" is primo material for the rumor mill. Without rumors about who's going over the edge, the art of conversation, as we gays know it, will cease to exist.

❖ Though all phobias, neuroses, and psychoses are good, nothing is trendier than old-fashioned paranoia. For a politically correct gay nervous breakdown to occur, there must be a demonstrable quotient of paranoia. See conspiracies everywhere. For those unsure about how to achieve p.c. paranoia, may I suggest consulting recent issues of the New York *Native*? The folks who coined the word "AIDSgate" aren't kidding around.

❖ If you do go for therapy, insist on group. Group therapy is the adult version of Show & Tell. I will never forgive the therapist who told me I was well. "Does that mean I can't go to group anymore?" I asked. Indeed it did. Group was great. Where else could I say, "Yes, George, I agree you are very disturbed, but let me show you a photo of my ex-lover and tell you what he did to me. Then you'll see that I am much crazier than you"?

❖ Cracking up takes precedence over everything else. Insanity is a full time job, and a great excuse to use to get out of doing things you don't want to do. Example: "I'd really like to meet your family, but, you see—well—I'm very upset right now. It's nothing, really, but Reginald is driving me nuts and I'm a tad suicidal." Or this version: "I'd really love to come up with a snappy wrap-up to this article, but today is not a good day. I'm really cracking up this time. Really. Have I told you what Tim Barrus did to me . . . ?"

5

Bloomingdale's Is A State Of Mind

The clothes! The Ralph Lauren polo shirts, the Halston suits, the Ultrasuede jackets, T-shirts of every hue, bleached fatigues and painter's pants, plaid shirts, transparent plastic belts, denim jackets and old corduroys, hooded sweat shirts, baseball caps, and shoes lined up under a forest of shoe trees on the floor; someone had once left the house and all he could talk about was that Malone had forty-four shoe trees in his closet. There were drawers and drawers of jump suits, shirts by Ronald Kolodzie, Estee Lauder lotions and astringents, and drawers and drawers of bathing suits, of which he had twenty-eight, in racing and boxer styles. . . . There was one drawer filled with nothing but thirty-seven T-shirts in different colors, colors he had bleached them or dyed them, soft plum and faded shrimp and celery green and all shades of yellow, his best color. . . . There was a closet hung with thirty-two plaid shirts, and a bureau filled entirely with jeans faded various shades of blue.

I finally stood up, depressed at all these things—for what were they but emblems of Malone's innocent heart, his inexhaustible desire to be liked?

—*Andrew Holleran*
Dancer From The Dance

If I didn't like him, I'd say that my friend Peter was the quintessential gay Yuppie. (Gyuppie? Guppie? They *used* to be Male JAPs.) The guy is trendy. Christ, he was a class act in *college*. Peter *knows* what to wear to this week's gay in-spot, what to serve for this season's perfect brunch, what tchatchkes should adorn this year's coffee table. He knows everything I don't. I wasn't surprised when the told me, "I went out last Saturday afternoon and just happened to be around Bloomingdale's. But then I realized that I'd forgotten my credit card. I felt almost . . . frightened. I don't suppose you'd understand that."

Sure I do. Being trendy is a process; you can never reach the point where you are able to declare "I *am* trendy" and have done with it. Trendiness demands constant vigilance. Slack off for just a few weeks and you'll find yourself eating in the wrong restaurant, shod in the wrong shoes, while, meanwhile, back at your apartment, your walls are whispering to each other about being in the wrong color. Even one missed opportunity to be trendy (one neglected issue of *New York* magazine, one skipped invite to M.K., one forgotten credit card) can have dire repercussions.

For those who labor ceaselessly in the fields of trendiness, there is but one constant, one comforting refuge, one oasis in the desert of continually shifting fashion. *Bloomingdale's!* O Bloomingdale's, thy very name is a delight! Thy wonders are myriad! Blessed be the joyfulness to be found in thy sanctums! Thou containeth all the perfumes of Araby (and Paris) to sweeten the little hands of thy shoppers! The quality of thy mercy is not restrained but droppeth like the gentle caviar of Beluga in thy gourmet food department! May those who deny thy name and worship Macy's be damned! Bloomingdale's! Thine is the kingdom and the power and the most adorable Calvin Kleins forever and ever.

Ironies—Intended and Unintended

The powers-that-be who suggested I write about Bloomingdale's were going after, I think, an ironic effect. My involvement in matters sadomasochistic and matters pornographic, my arch declaration that while I knew there was an Upper East Side to the island of Manhattan, I had certainly never been there—to say nothing about my decidedly untrendy appearance (I look like I was once fond of 1971 and decided to stay there)—would create, it was believed, I believe, a marked contrast between what I am and what I am writing about here. Out of The Pleasure Chest and into better dresses. Darker motives may also have been afoot in assigning me to cover Bloomingdale's; sending someone who was at home at the Mineshaft to the *au courant* holy of holies might be a vilely sadistic enactment of the favorite editorial game, "Now I've got him, the—I can't say it, but it rhymes with rich."

Ha, ha. The sad fact (to me, *now*) is that a number of years ago I actually lived on the Upper East Side and was no stranger to Bloomingdale's. I tried to be a Bloomingdale's queen. I really did. I made the requisite pilgrimages on all the holy days of obligation—Saturday afternoons, paydays, every day in December. I charged. I socialized gaily in the men's room. I tried. I failed. I just didn't have the strength of character to make it into the trendy 400,000. I began to doubt the system: the vase ($145) *was* divine; it would look wonderful on the simple little "put it *anywhere*" table imported from Brazil ($275), but in my heart, I didn't *want* the vase—or the table I already owned.

The Unreal Thing

When I began to criticize Bloomingdale's, I began to question a state of mind. No other store in America has the mystique Bloomie's has. Perhaps Neiman-Marcus comes closest, but Neiman-Marcus is a parody of affluence. Those outrageously expensive trinkets in the Neiman-Marcus Christmas catalog ($250,000 for one dead animal, a swimming pool in the shape of your initials, his and her submarines)—coupled with Neiman-Marcus's insistence that these items do sell—are so far removed from the reality most of us experience, they're absurdly, mordantly funny. The Neiman-Marcus catalog almost always shows up in features on TV news and/or in *People* magazine, entertainment for the masses, *Dallas* reduced to glossy four-color.

But not *real,* accessible, enticing. Bloomingdale's isn't the dream world of Neiman-Marcus. Bloomingdale's is an artificial value system.

What would *Pravda* say about Bloomingdale's? If Bloomingdale's isn't the epitome of capitalist decadence, nothing is. But, as I write—at Christmas—'tis the season to be jolly, not to do Marxist deconstructions on Bloomingdale's. A great many gay people will spend a great deal of money this December in Bloomingdale's. It's a truism in retail that fully one-quarter of the year's sales are realized in the month before Christmas. Bloomingdale's is selling what gay people want; it is impossible to discuss the gay sensibility without discussing Bloomingdale's.

At Bloomingdale's the individual items themselves seem almost beside the point. The main attraction is the cumulative effect but Bloomingdale's is, strangely enough, less a triumph of mise-en-scene than of montage: we cut mentally from item to item. Bloomingdale's can't be taken in all at once; there's too much there—thousands of neckties, endless variations on the theme of pots and pans, millions of twinkling gems. The images don't stop coming, and now that Bloomingdale's has "gone video," there are countless shifting photos of items to accompany the items themselves. Bloomingdale's can be a dizzying experience, a series of shock cuts, like the Odessa steps sequence from *Potemkin.* In the pre-Christmas mania, Bloomingdale's seems to be devoted to full frontal attack.

The Elegantly Useless

Though Bloomingdale's doesn't completely neglect the utilitarian—you can, for example, buy an inexpensive crock pot or certain items of clothing (Lacoste shirts, etc.) sacrosanct to the Preppie—shopping in Bloomingdale's is principally supposed to be entertaining, like going to Great Adventure. Bloomingdale's is the opposite of K-Mart and Sears, stores of such overwhelming practicality, they reduce shopping to a task, like washing the dishes. You can have a good time, an afternoon's treat, at Bloomingdale's. The sheer silliness of many of the items available and the fervor of shoppers pursuing these items provide the bizarre charm that makes Bloomingdale's "like no other store in the world."

In Judith Krantz's roman-a-dreck *Scruples* (which, oddly enough, is not merely what the characters lack, but also the name of the department store that figures prominently in the novel), a distraught woman comes to the store manager with a problem: she needs to spend at least $200 on a gift for her despised mother-in-law and hasn't a clue what to buy. (My details may be off; I haven't the fortitude to go through *Scruples* to find the actual wording.) Happily, the manager has *the* answer: a silver walnut crusher. I have no doubt that similar scenes occur hundreds of times a day at Bloomingdale's. My favorite Bloomie's story concerns one of my former college professors who proudly announced to her class that she had found after a long search the perfect Xmas present for her father in Bloomingdale's: an electric cherry pitter. I can identify with Dr. Cherry Pitter. I once bought my mother a pewter toothpick holder in the shape of a porcupine in good ol' Bloomie's. Get it? The picks served as the porcupine's quills. Mumsy loved it.

Fans of the elegantly useless will not be disappointed in Bloomingdale's this Christmas. It was very difficult to pick my favorite item from the literally millions of competing doodads. The $285 wine decanter in the shape of a sick duck, the $35 monogrammed American Empress card bathtowel (the catalog calls it "a credit to any bathroom"; the copywriter should be shot), the $15 pair of black lacquered teak chopsticks with rests were all lovely, strong contenders. But since these items have *some* purpose, I was ultimately won over by the $155 sterling silver quill pen and miniature glass inkwell with sterling hinged top. Stephen Sondheim's song "The Ladies Who Lunch" (from *Company*) notes ladies "looking grim/Cause they've been sitting/Choosing a hat/Does anyone still wear a hat?" Well, some do, but *no one* uses a $155 sterling silver quill pen and miniature glass inkwell with sterling hinged top. From England. Order item No. 393191. From Bloomingdale's By Mail, 115 Brand Road, Salem VA 24156. Add $5 shipping and handling. New York and Virginia residents add sales tax. Add $4.50 for gift wrap.

Bloomingdale's and Gay Men

In the movie *Garbo Talks*, the very gay character who Harvey Fierstein plays admits to working at Alexander's and prides himself because he didn't lie and say he worked for Bloomingdale's. The connection between Bloomingdale's and gay men is so strong and so widely known that it's joke material. "What's the biggest gay bar in the world?" "Bloomingdale's." Yet Bloomingdale's only has fifteen stores in nine states, mostly in the Northeast urban megalopolis (four stores in New York, two each in New Jersey, Massachusetts, and Pennsylvania; one each in Connecticut, Virginia, and Maryland.) A planned expansion will up the total to seventeen stores in ten states; still no comparison to, say, the hundreds of Jefferson Ward stores. It is not physical access to the store, but the idea of Bloomingdale's that's part of the national gay consciousness. This article could play in a gay paper in Peoria; an article about Jordan Marsh or Bamberger's, second-string Bloomingdale's, could not. Editors of nationally circulated gay mags have told me to "watch" (i.e., omit) references that "they" (i.e., the great unwashed "out there," not within two hundred miles of New York City) wouldn't get, but Bloomingdale's, that most parochial of stores, is something every fag understands.

Though all gays (and many straights) realize that Bloomingdale's has a special place in the hearts and check books of urban male homosexuals, Bloomingdale's remains officially oblivious to gays. Bloomingdale's doesn't go out of its way to solicit the gay male dollar—no ads in the gay press, no corporate contributions to gay-related charities or organizations, no cute little floats in the Gay Pride Parade. (A mailing from the Mineshaft about its Mr. Leather contest noted that any company, "even Bloomingdale's," could sponsor a contestant; Bloomingdale's chose not to.) But even to the untrained eye, Bloomingdale's could hardly be accused of discriminating against gays. On my recent visits to Bloomingdale's, gay shoppers were out in droves, purchasing all sorts of goodies from gay salespeople, items that the possibly gay buyer knew, just *knew*, would go over big with members of the tribe. But Bloomingdale's corporate policy toward gays is benign neglect.

Some years back, it was rumored that the store had sent out a memo denying a gay connection, but I can find no record of this document. A number of people employed by Bloomingdale's claim to have heard of this memo; no one has seen it. And Bloomingdale's isn't talking. Bloomingdale's doesn't talk about gays; it doesn't talk about blacks or Jews or Albanians either. It does talk about customers. It likes them.

What I find most extraordinary about Bloomingdale's is its ability to promote itself above and beyond the usual forms of advertising. A Bloomingdale's brochure states, "Bloomingdale's is a dynamic leader in the discovery and merchandising of fashions for men and women from the foremost designers through the use of promotion, advertising, display and publicity." That's putting it mildly. The brochure continues, "The resulting media coverage has been unusual, ranging from a *Time* magazine cover story to a section in *People* magazine to two separate 15 minute segments on the television show *60 Minutes*." The film industry perceives Bloomingdale's as a New York institution and the store has been involved in such films as *Manhattan, Starting Over, An Unmarried Woman, Splash, Moscow On The Hudson*, and *9½ Weeks*." That's not quite correct. Bloomingdale's perceives *itself* as a New York institution and hardly greets filmmakers with open arms. Films which are not sufficiently big-budget will not be given permission to shoot in the store. (Though Bloomingdale's is more receptive to letting its shopping bags, which it calls "an art form" it "pioneered," show up in films.) Neither will films which might portray Bloomingdale's unfavorably. It was okay for Burt Reynolds to have an anxiety attack in *Starting Over* in the store and for Robin Williams in *Moscow On The Hudson* to defect there, but it was not okay for Ali McGraw and Alan King to have a knock-down fight in Bloomie's in *Just Tell Me What You Want*. (The scene was filmed in Bergdorf's after Bloomingdale's nixed it.) But did Bloomie's read *9½ Weeks*? It's a bizarre chronicle of an S/M relationship; I can't wait to see what was filmed in Bloomingdale's.*

---

*Not much as it turned out.

Bloomingdale's As News

Bloomingdale's has the uncanny knack of making itself news. Who can forget that thrilling day in 1976 when Queen Elizabeth decided to drop in and Bloomingdale's president Marvin Traub managed to get the traffic reversed on Lexington Avenue (because the Queen can only exit a vehicle from the right), making front page news? More recently, the New Jersey section of the *Times* of November 11, 1984 carried a story entitled "Bloomingdale's 'Nights' Go On":

> *When the guests pulled up to Bloomingdale's here [Short Hills] for a recent black-tie extravaganza, they were greeted by lion dancers cavorting in authentic costumes to the beat of an Oriental drummer.*
>
> *The men and women, who had paid $350 a couple to attend, also were greeted by kimono-clad Japanese-American hostesses distributing programs.*
>
> *The delicate, haunting ping, ping, ping of background music was provided by two Japanese musicians, one playing the koto, a six-foot-long string instrument, and the other a shakuhachi, a reed flute.*

The story, which continues for an incredible seventeen paragraphs, has no news content, but was presented as news, not disguised as a "What To Buy For Christmas" feature. When you spend as much money advertising in the *Times* (at about $8000 a page) as Bloomingdale's does, I suppose you are entitled to an occasional free ad-as-news. And where else but at Bloomingdale's would an appearance by some of the performers in *Dynasty* (to publicize a line of *Dynasty* clothes) cause a near riot. And lots of "news" stories, too. Joan Collins wasn't even there. In person, that is; her images were displayed in the windows. One window showed Krystle surrounded by a number of representations of Alexis; another showed Alexis surrounded by Krystles.

The *Dynasty*/Bloomingdale's madness of November 18 made page four of the *Daily News* (in an article by Larry Sutton who, trivia buffs take note, was my very first editor way back on a high school newspaper). Bloomingdale's "declined to comment" on the incident. If Bloomingdale's won't talk to the *Daily News*, do you think they'd tell *me* anything? Grow up.

Let's Dish

That's not quite true. Bloomie's would talk; the problem was what they'd talk *about*. The store loves its things. It has *lots* of exciting plans for the future. This Christmas is just so thrilling. Bloomie's and I just don't speak the same language. I had no idea what questions to ask: What's new in the wonderful world of wicker? How's Anne Klein? Just what color is teal anyway? My worst nightmare was about to come true: I would be put into a room of a thousand demented interior designers, all of whom knew my furniture was bought on sale at Kaufmann.

"Is there an ultimate Bloomingdale's item?" I asked one employee. "Something that expresses the ur-text of the store." "We have many beautiful items," he said, not quite understanding what I was asking, but much too polite, too Bloomingdale's-ish, to say, "What the fuck are you talking about?" People who work for Bloomingdale's and serious Bloomingdale's shoppers didn't trust me enough to offer any criticisms of the store. I was, after all, not "one of them." I was an unspending wallflower at the buying orgy.

The typical Bloomingdale's customer is a cliché. Nine years ago, *Time* wrote that the store's clientele was "young, affluent, fashion-conscious, traveled, professional people. They are attuned . . . to clothes of fashion and quality, stereo equipment and wacky gadgetry for the compact Manhattan society of small apartments, crowded schedules and casual relationships. . . . This market, Bloomingdale's has learned, enjoys tasting but does not stand still long enough to savor. It thrives on variety and excitement." Those people—*those exact same people*—are still in there shopping. Manhattan will one day sink from the weight of objects d'Bloomingdale's cluttering up those small apartments.

Contrary to rumor, you don't have to be a gay male to shop in Bloomingdale's. The store is full of fags because a good number of gay men fit the profile of the customer that Bloomingdale's caters to. It would be impossible (and probably horrifying) to calculate how many gay people are spending how much money each year in the store. It seems pretty obvious that if gays boycotted Bloomingdale's, the store's profits would drop considerably. But gays would never boycott Bloomingdale's even if the store became wildly homophobic. The type of gays Bloomingdale's attracts are not generally known for a developed gay political consciousness; they are the ones who voted for Reagan in 1984 because they *were* better off then than they were four years before.

Bloomingdale's, History Of

Founded by Lyman and Joseph Bloomingdale in 1872, the store's first "first" was the "sky carriage," (an elevator); it was the first store in New York to have such a contraption. But until the end of World War II, Bloomingdale's was a fairly conventional store. Then I.E. Davidson, the store's boss from 1947 until 1967, dropped refrigerators and other major appliances; the big push was on to make Bloomie's a never-ending party. You can't buy a bar of Ivory soap in Bloomingdale's; you can buy Japanese Rice Soap, Italian Milk Soap, European Lavender Soap, Bavarian Cameo Soap, French Mont St. Michel Soap, East Indies Spice Soap, and Chinese Jasmine Soap. No to Johnson's Baby Shampoo, but yes to "our new brew of Blooming Ale [sic] suds, beer shampoo that's on tap for a marvelous holiday gift." It's ten bucks. Even items that sold well (but generated little profit) such as records were phased out. From a marketing standpoint, it makes perfect sense. Why sell a Bic cigarette lighter when the same sales space can be given to "Holiday fire works—the two-in-one Savanna lighter [that] does more than merely set a heart aflame. It also boasts all the tools of the trade: knife, screwdriver, opener, butterfly nut driver, spanners, scale, and rule"? The Bloomingdale's shopper doesn't want a Bic lighter anyway. Bloomingdale's is a retailer's version of social Darwinism: survival of the priciest or, a bit more accurately, of the highest profit margin.

"The annual Bloomingdale's country promotions have evolved into an eagerly awaited cultural, as well as merchandising, event." In 1977, the first major "country promotion" (there were minor promotions of Italy and France in 1960 and 1961) "celebrated" India. India was again "on" for 1986. Am I the only one to feel queasy about these "celebrations" of India? A friend of mine who's in the import business moved his operations from Taiwan to India "in time for Bloomingdale's" because of the obscenely cheap labor to be found there. "There" as in India, not as in Bloomie's. ("The unions are starting to get into Taiwan.") India, a country wracked by violence and starvation, will once again be acclaimed by Bloomingdale's, America's capital of "let them eat brioche." *60 Minutes* recently reported that women in India, if their families are unable to provide them with sufficient dowries, are routinely slaughtered. American women, thanks to Bloomingdale's, will soon be acclaiming India for "all its cute things."

Trends

But Bloomingdale's flagship store at 1000 Third Avenue in Manhattan has more on its mind than profit. Most of Bloomingdale's profit comes from its branch stores; Manhattan exists to provide Bloomingdale's most sacred maxim: "Image Is Substance." (Which sounds like it should be right up there with "Ignorance Is Strength.") In a *New York Times Magazine* article on Bloomingdale's, Jesse Kornbluth wrote:

> *[I]mage comes straight from Manhattan. Its market share here, its reputation for value or status, its ability to define a mood and then translate it in communities radically different from New York—these are the tests of retailing vitality today.*

> *If image has become almost more important than the merchandise, it may be because most of the major stores offer much the same thing.*
> *. . .[In the late 1960s] some visionary merchants— particularly Bloomingdale's chairman, Marvin Traub— attempted to make shopping at their stores a trend in itself. They promoted designer clothes for label-conscious consumers*

who found at least a part of their identities in the products they bought. But . . . that formula worked too well. No store has an "'exclusive" on big-volume designers anymore: Calvin Klein, Ralph Lauren, and Anne Klein are sold everywhere. "Basically, we've all got the same bridge hand," says Macy's senior vice president of stores, Michael Stemen. "The variable is presentation."

In this trend-eat-trend world, for Bloomingdale's to be truly trendy, it must invent the trends and not merely pick up on them. Today, Japan is chic; next year, it will be Scandinavia and Italy who'll take the honors. In 1986, the images of what's hot that Bloomingdale's will be pushing came from one of the most desperately troubled countries in the world. After India, what will they do for an encore? Ethiopia?

Marvin Traub once remarked, "We are not only in competition with other stores, but with the Guggenheim and the Met." Traub's arrogance is sadly on target. In culturally and morally impoverished America, shopping *is* art. More people appreciate the beauty of a Bloomingdale's display than appreciate the beauty of a Picasso. No less than that spokesperson for the stylishly useless, Lee Radziwill, told *Time* magazine in its cover story on Bloomingdale's (the first and only store to be so featured), "It's the obvious place to go for *everything.*"

The Smell of Money

Some of the statistics about Bloomingdale's are mind-boggling. On an average Saturday, some 60,000 people will visit the Manhattan store (many more on a December Saturday; somewhat less on an August Saturday). Each square foot of Bloomingdale's generates four times more sales per year than is the average for a U.S. department store. Bloomingdale's may be earning as much as 5 cents after-tax profit per each sales dollar—phenomenal for a retail business. Bloomingdale's is one of New York's major tourist attractions, as popular as the Statue of Liberty. A friend from California says that when he visits New York, "I may not always go to the theatre, but I always go to Bloomingdale's."

Should the eyes get overwhelmed by the images at Bloomingdale's, the nose can take over. The smells from the cosmetics department seem to permeate the store. The odor is unique. Since it is made up of thousands of different cosmetics (and the smell of money), it is everything—and nothing—at once: olfactory overkill. Which is as it should be. After all, there's a war going on between fiercely competitive cosmetics manufacturers.

In an article on the cosmetics business, *Forbes* magazine called Bloomingdale's "The premier battleground of the industry." One buyer noted, "Every cosmetics buyer in the country comes to New York twice a year. Before she goes out to Brooklyn to visit her mother, she stops at Bloomingdale's to see what's new." Some of the details about the never-ending lip gloss wars are perversely fascinating. Ads for particular cosmetics are laid out by Bloomingdale's, with Bloomingdale's name in large letters at the bottom, though the manufacturer pays in full for the ad. (Bloomingdale's does not pass its volume discount ad rate along to the manufacturer.) About half of Bloomingdale's high traffic main floor is given over to cosmetics. *Where* a manufacturer's wares are displayed is given absurd importance. After Revlon annoyed Bloomingdale's, it was "demoted"—moved from the middle of the floor to against the wall, "no woman's land." To get reinstated into Bloomingdale's good graces, Revlon went financially bananas in its support of a Bloomingdale's promotion.

Back in my younger days when I worked "real" jobs, I was mostly involved in the retail business. (I am really letting out all my darkest secrets in this essay, ain't I?) Retailing, like hairdressing, is an exercise in allocating a great deal of time and effort to essentially minor matters. The cosmetics war is one example. Another is the fact that the hours of planning and discussion and departmental in-fighting that go into a store window display are always out-of-synch with whatever the results might be. Bloomingdale's once sent a troubleshooter to the Roquefort caves in France to see what could be done to make the cheese less salty. But the French—to their credit—weren't about to overturn hundreds of years of tradition for Bloomingdale's. But Marvin

Traub was successful in persuading a Holland chocolate company to change the colors on its packaging. You can just imagine the size of the intercontinental phone bills that went into *that* monumental undertaking.

At Bloomingdale's, more than at any other store in the country (though Macy's is steadily gaining), trendy aesthetics take center (and only) stage. The *Times* reported:

> *So department stores, normally a stable underpinning of the city's business life, are suddenly emerging as news-making hybrids: part store, part theater, part center for continuing education. And because these institutions are, increasingly, the personal projections of a few key executives, the men and women who run them have assumed a degree of celebrity—and wealth—unknown to their predecessors. These executives may earn as much as $500,000 a year, salaries that reflect their multifaceted roles as merchants, curators and social philosophers.*

But the Bloomingdale's aesthetic is essentially empty. The store's "curators" preside only over treasures with price tags affixed to them. The store's "social philosophers" are not concerned with Substance and Meaning, but with Style and Vacuity. In my most recent visits to Bloomingdale's I kept flashing on a line from Robert Patrick's play *T-Shirts*: "When a society's only values are good looks and money, sooner or later people are going to wind up exchanging the one for the other." Should Bloomingdale's wish to use that line in a future promotion, I'll send them a bill for a finder's fee.

6

How To Cruise The Met

It's Not Just For Opera Anymore

A few weeks ago a friend was giving me one of the twice-weekly installments of his *Tales of Woe* (which, now that I think of it, resemble a version of *Dynasty* in which all the roles are played by Joan Collins) when he launched into one of his favorite recurring motifs: the shortage of gay men in the Americas. Though empirically absurd, this topic is nevertheless one of the most dominant (and most submissive) themes in gay history. A typical expression of it goes something like: "It's impossible to meet people. I'm not really looking for a lover, but I'd like to meet *someone*. Forget the bars. After twenty years in the bars—did I say twenty?—I meant ten—I'm *over* alcoholics, clique queens, and writers, present company excepted. And now that we're not allowed to go to the baths anymore without being made to feel like Typhoid Mary, what's left? Don't suggest the personal ads—I still blame you, T.R., for the '30ish hunky adventurer' who turned out to be a sixty-two-year-old, three-hundred-pound Mafia hit-man who answered to the name of Baby Death. I'm too old to cruise the streets, too broke to afford a gay, gay, gay vacation, and everybody else at work is more fucked up than I am. There must be someplace to go to meet intelligent, employed, nice gay men."

Sure there is. It's called the Metropolitan Opera House and on any given night (except Sundays) from September to April, the place is loaded with faggots. Even if only 10% of the Met's audience is actively gay, at least another 10% is passively gay, and then there are those gays who can't make up their minds, those supermarket queens, the A/Ps. Anyway, the Met's a big place, so however you figure things like this (is a bisexual counted as being half-gay or three-quarters-queer?), it's fairly safe to assume that there are a lot of gays at the Met. Even dismissing those gays who are ineligible due to prior commitments, offensive shoes, and incorrect opinions of Ghena Dimitrova, an evening at the Met will still place you in close proximity to *tons* of gays ready, willing, and able to make your bed more crowded. And a faggot you encounter at the Met isn't likely to be a mere dicklicker. Met gays tend to be college-educated, self-support-ing, and well-behaved, smart, relatively affluent, nice dicklick-ers. Most Met queens could wear signs: "I can be taken to meet your mother without causing undue *tsuris* in Poughkeepsie."

Opera queens have gotten a bad press. They are thought to be cruelly bitchy, horrendously petty, and extraordinarily demanding. And they *are*. But at the same time they aren't the sort who'll throw up on you at bars, think Monsterrat Caballé is something you order in a French restaurant, or insist that they move in with you immediately after—or even during—the first fuck. Opera queens are probably the closest approximations to responsible adults one is likely to encounter in one's journey through gay life.

The negative image of the opera queen is largely due to the negative image of opera. Opera is thought to be a lot of fat people wandering around bizarre locales singing in foreign languages for many tedious hours. And it *is*. But, then again, a gay bar is a lot of drunk people wandering around bizarre locales either saying nothing or speaking in tongues for many tedious hours so it's not like going to the opera for the first time will be an entirely brand new experience for the typical cock-sucker. Going to the opera is really very much like going to a gay bar (alcohol is available at the Met for those gays who are constitutionally unable to cruise without clutching a drink), only at the opera you can sit down for long stretches of time and even nod off without being thought a party pooper. (Best time for naps: the second act of *Aida*, all of *Francesca da Rimini* except the intermissions, whenever Venus is off-stage in *Tannhaeuser*, and during arias sung by Renata Scotto.)

If you are going to start cruising the Met (and you really should—you owe it to yourself and the Met needs the money: Hildegard Behrens doesn't come cheap, no matter what she looks like), there are a few things you should know:

A) Forget old movies that show operagoers dressed in tuxedos and evening gowns. Despite whatever urges you have to wear an evening gown—and no matter how elegantly simple the dress—remember that except for the Met's opening night (which is terrible for cruising anyway), formal attire is only worn by tourists (i.e., people who read the libretto during the performance; it's okay, however, to follow the score—but learning to read music seems a very high price to pay when all you're essentially after is a wee bit of culture and a big dick). Reverse-chic is very trendy. You should try to look like you see going to an opera as a come-as-you-are party, something you just sort of show up for without paying it much thought. (Placido Domingo does this all the time when he's *in* the opera being performed, not merely *at* it.) Leather is permitted, sometimes even encouraged, and, occasionally, such as at performances of *Die Walküre*, demanded.

B) It is helpful to learn a few technical words that will enable you to converse fluently with opera queens. Now, watch my lips: "Of course, if you're the sort of person who likes that type of soprano (so-*pran*-o). . . ." "Marvelous voice, but you know she's a lesbian (*lez*-bi-an), don't you?" "If he can get through this role, I'm Marie of Rumania (Roo-*ma*-ni-a)" "How about stopping for a drink at my apartment (a-*part*-ment)?"

C) Cruising the Met is a team, not an individual, sport. Though there is no law that says you can't go solo to the opera, a man alone at the opera is usually perceived to be a weird heterosexual. Lord knows you have enough problems without getting a reputation for *that*. (To answer your obvious question—Christ, I have to tell you fairies *everything*, don't I?: you start an opera queen team by having a few friends read this essay. No, Mary, you *don't* show them your copy; you send each selected sister out to buy his very own copy. An excessive pass-on rate doesn't mean shit when we come right down to the central reason for my telling you all this neat stuff: getting me more money based on increased sales of *Kvetch* by addressing the issue most readers are most concerned about—getting laid more.) Where was I? Oh yes, opera queens are pack animals, but mating is never done within the pack. The way it works: someone in your pack knows someone in another pack, everybody gets introduced to everybody else, pair bonds are formed, and people marry and die without ever learning the plot of *Il Trovatore*.

D) Since the most successful cruising is done during intermissions (the Met is famous for long intermissions, often longer than the performance itself—*they know*), never, ever, attend an opera that doesn't have an intermission. *Elektra* and *Wozzeck* are cute enough, but hopeless for cruising.

E) When in doubt, criticize. Ignorance of opera is no excuse for holding your tongue. Even if you think High C is a fruit drink, don't know the difference between Tosca and Wotan, and couldn't hum "La donna e mobile" if your life depended on it, you can still be an opera critic: pick on the sets, the costumes, and the physical appearances of the singers (how fat is she?); knowingly intone "Well, she *has* been better"; kvetch about other audience members—"Yes, darlings, all through Isolde's Narration and Curse, this woman in front of me was chewing gum—what will the peasants do next?" When all else fails, lament the passing of Maria Callas.

F) Opera queens are very receptive to newcomers in their midst and eager to share their knowledge of opera, but don't needlessly annoy them. After witnessing two hundred-plus performances of *Carmen*, you won't be in much of a mood to have your mind fucked with either. Some things *not* to say:

At *Madame Butterfly*—"Funny, she doesn't look Japanese."
At *Tristan und Isolde*—"Isn't he *ever* going to die?"
At *Der Rosenkavalier*—"What is this? A dyke opera?"

At just about anything: "Since you know she's going to kill herself at the end, why don't we skip the last act and go fuck?"

G) Some operas attract more gays than others. Operas in German, operas longer than four hours, operas featuring famous fading divas are big favorites. Put these criteria all together and they spell *Parsifal*, which is where all nice opera queens spend Good Friday.

H) Though opera queens are on the ladylike side, there is no need to test them on this too strenuously. Without a chaperon, I, for one, wouldn't be caught dead with an opera queen in a parterre box at the Met.

I) Years spent in the company of characters famous for going mad at the drop of a handkerchief and ingenious in their suicide methods have given some opera queens rather, er, distinctive ideas about what sex is. Before you become, er, intimate with an opera queen, it is best to query him thoroughly about his tastes in sex lest you wind up being entombed or placed on a rock and surrounded by impenetrable fire. A little bondage is nifty, but draw the line at being placed in a burlap sack. Under no circumstances whatsoever go to a bullfight with an opera queen. Novices to opera should also be wary about an opera queen who asks, "Before we do it, would you like to try to answer a few riddles?" And run for the nearest exit when your request for a little kiss is met with "This is a kiss according to Tosca."

Cruising the Met is probably the most respectable way to meet fellow faggots. Being able to answer "At Jessye Norman's first Met *Ariadne auf Naxos*" instead of "At Sleaze Night at the baths" to the question "And where did you two meet?" not only sounds classy but helps keep up the myth of the homosexual as appreciator of life's "finer things." (There is never any need to mention that after *Ariadne auf Naxos*, you both tramped off to the baths to consummate your relationship.)

Now you may be saying, "O great sage, T.R., after I meet the great love of my life by cruising the Met just like you told me, does that mean I have to continue going to the opera forever? Frankly, darling, between you and me, I can't stand opera."

Fear not, dear, I have some great news for you: the most serious of serious opera queens never go to the opera at all! Why the opera queen's opera queen Ethan Mordden himself (honey, that child writes books on opera!) once announced (*Philadelphia Gay News*, January 24, 1985): "All the opera we have been getting recently is so boring I can't sit through a performance. . . . I no longer care about going to the opera." What's good enough for Ethan is good enough for you.

See you girls at a revival of *Stop Making Sense*.

7

THE COMPLEAT
A-GAY
Or, the Social Caste System
in Gay America

The social caste system in gay America did not die with Truman Capote. It's alive and well and being lushly nourished in an artificial nursery called Manhattan. Just living there guarantees the loss of a few I.Q. points each year, so you've got to do something to pass the time before you wake up at brunch one Sunday and discover you're ninety. So New York faggots have invented a social game as elaborate as it is vague. It's not the biggest gay game in town; it's the only gay game in town.

Think of Manhattan gay society as The War of the Spanish Succession—a long, expensive contretemps that nobody wins and that few people outside of the struggle even care about. At the top of the hierarchy are the empresses who map out the strategy. These are the feared and despised (but nevertheless admired) *A-Gays*. Keeping your status as an A-Gay depends on your address, the color of your American Express card, and at least one mention a year in an important gossip column. (Liz Smith's, preferably, though Suzy will do; Michael Musto's column has yet to prove itself, so A-Gays are wary of it, and a mention in the *New York Native* will cause an A-Gay to fire his press agent.) Nothing else counts.

The Others

Next to the A-Gays are the queens whom the A-Gays jocularly call *Fun Gays*—those border neighbors who don't care about their social status as long as they're having a good time. Fun Gays often enter A-Gay territory for periods of designated truce.

And finally, at the bottom of the heap, there are the *B-Gays*, composed of princesses who try too hard, shop incorrectly, sit in the Family Circle at the Met, and, unlike the Fun Gays, are worried about not being A-Gays. A-Gays and some Fun Gays are ambitious, but B-Gays are desperate. Below the B-Gays are the peasants, who theoretically don't exist at all.

To be an A-Gay you *must*:

❖ Live on the Upper East Side of Manhattan (57th to 86th St., only, *please*). Some other areas of the city are acceptable, but great care must be exercised if one is an A-Gay who doesn't live on the Upper East Side. Certain buildings on the West Side (with views of the park) are okay, as are some Chelsea brownstones and some Soho lofts, but these are vastly outnumbered by the wrong buildings. Residence in a wrong building in an incorrect section of the city will doom you forever to B-Gayhood. An A-Gay would rather give up his Porthault sheets than live in Brooklyn Heights, Hoboken or Jersey City—though Fun Gays can live in these places and be thought "charmingly eccentric." In the A-Gay mind, Long Island is what one passes through to get to the Pines. With the exception of Key West and San Francisco and wherever Mumsy and Daddy live, an A-Gay considers the rest of the country to be simply "out there." (Provincetown, incidentally, is regarded by A-Gays as a haven for B-Gays and down-on-their-luck Fun Gays.)

❖ Carry on your person *at all times* a Platinum Amex Card. No other credit card matters in the least. Even the lowest B-Gay can get Visa.

❖ Hold A-Gay opinions. The A-Gay writer (who's "one of us, darling") is Harvey Fierstein (because he's the richest; A-Gays *adore* former Fun Gays who make it big). The A-Gay TV show is *Masterpiece Theater* (ditto). The A-Gay newspaper is the

Times (But only on Sundays and only for the Arts and Leisure and Real Estate sections; most serious A-Gays get these sections delivered by messenger on the Thursday preceding cover date). The A-Gay singer is *still* Judy Garland (Liza Minnelli is passable, but don't push her too much). The A-Gay musical is *still A Chorus Line* (saying something good about *The Phantom of the Opera* will brand you as an upstart, perhaps a very far-out Fun Gay, probably a pushy B-Gay, but definitely not A). The A-Gay department store is *still* Bloomingdale's (though an *occasional* browse through Macy's will be tolerated). A-Gays tend to find a group opinion and then they all stick with it. Though A-Gays consider it their sworn duty to know what is *au courant* and what is *outre*, they will ultimately die praising only Garland, *A Chorus Line*, and Bloomingdale's.

What else? Oh yes, the A-Gay sex magazine is *Guys* (largely because its editor, Jerry Douglas, is an A-Gay mascot). The A-Gay old movie is *Gone With The Wind* (but when A-Gays are being silly—the favorite method of relieving the stress of being an A-Gay—they will recite all the dialogue from *The Wizard Of Oz*). The A-Gay Bible is *Miss Manners' Guide To Excruciatingly Correct Behavior* (even though A-Gays consider Judith Martin to be somewhat *arriviste*). The A-Gay European country is France (England *only* for a weekend; Italy, provided that one is staying in a friend's villa). The A-Gay island (A-Gays do not consider Manhattan an island; they consider it the world) is probably Eleuthera or St. Croix (but, since A-Gays don't know much about geography, they generally just announce they're "off to the islands"; Cozumel—once a great favorite among A-Gays—has fallen into disfavor with them now because too many Bs go there). Don't you love all this?

The Working A-Gay

For an A-Gay who must work (say, if Daddy disowned him over that silly business with Raoul—luckily Mumsy still sends occasional checks and she'll outlive the old bastard, anyway), there are A-Gay professions: lawyers, investment bankers, some types of doctors (Ph.D.s, ophthalmologists, psychiatrists are good, but gynecologists, pediatricians and urologists are too messy), and high-middle executives for "nice" (i.e., Fortune 500) companies. Interior designing and hairdressing are iffy; there are too many B-Gays in those occupations. Exceptions are made for gays who "do" the apartment or the hair of a *major* A-Gay celebrity, like Chita Rivera or Joan Collins. And if you have so much as *touched* Jackie O's couch or neck, you are forever an A-Gay. (Oddly—nothing is ever simple in the world of A-Gays—while Jackie O elevates all the gays around her to A-Gayness, any A-Gay who has anything to do with Nancy Reagan is immediately stripped of social status. A-Gays can be very tough.)

An error *commonly* made about A-Gays is that money *alone* makes an A-Gay. This used to be true and is still *somewhat* true (there are no poor A-Gays), but as one notable A-Gay, who requested that I not use his name (A-Gays tend to be on the shy side) explained, "Money makes one rich. But money, accompanied by social power, exquisite taste, a measure of achievement, savoir-faire, good connections, wit and charm makes one an A-Gay." See how easy it is?

If you aren't an A-Gay, some people (mainly the *very* A-Gay) think you might as well be dead. But don't despair. You may fit in further down the line. Fun Gays don't exactly sit home nights, and many also wind up in Liz Smith's column. One of the great ironies of this game is that, while it is damn near impossible to be an A-Gay without money, it is damn near equally impossible to be a Fun Gay *with* money. Money can't buy happiness, but it can buy fun. This is why A-Gays and Fun Gays need each other.

It's pretty much of a hard and fast rule that Fun Gays must be "creative." Artists, writers, actors, musicians, photographers, directors—even window dressers, chefs, DJ's, models, producers, and an occasional waiter—are all considered "creative." But note: to *be creative* it is not necessary that you actually *do* anything creative. Many of the most creative actors have never technically set foot on a stage. Some extraordinarily creative photographers wouldn't know a lens opening from a Broadway opening. Here, image and self-promotion count more than actual achievement. Fun Gays are, well, fun. Since every A-Gay sees himself as a potential Gertrude Stein discovering a Picasso, A-Gays like Fun Gays. Fun Gays, according to As, "brighten up a party so wonderfully." However, when A-Gays are not in mixed company (i.e., when there are no non-As present), their favorite topics of conversation are the excesses of the Fun Gays: "Personally, I think he goes a bit too far in his writing, but other people [code for "non-As"] seem to like that sort of thing;" "I still think that that S/M business is quite strange;" "He's utterly lovely and I enjoy buying him dinner—poor dear never has any money—but I'm not sure his acting career is working out."

B-Gays

If all else fails, there are always the B-Gays. B-Gays include such folks as fags in real estate, cute clothing salesmen, art gallery proprietors, antique dealers, and owners of gay bars. (Occasionally, when a bar is particularly hot, the owner is elevated to A-Gayhood for the duration of the bar's popularity.) Please note that there is no such thing as a gay bartender. That gentleman behind the bar in a gay establishment is assuredly a singer or a dancer or a porno star tending to customers' requests "just to help the owner out"—a Fun Gay if ever there was one. Just about everyone who doesn't live on Manhattan is *de facto* a B-Gay unless he's a Fun Gay who once in a while really does create something (which may, in fact, be the reason he doesn't live on Manhattan). To the extent that they are acknowledged, lesbians are B-Gays.

As with anything else, there are exceptions to this structure. *Great* wealth makes *anyone* an A-Gay. A person can live in a bad building in Sri Lanka, loathe opera, be heterosexual, but if he has a hundred million dollars or so—he *is* an A-Gay. Likewise, an impoverished, talentless gay with only twelve inches of cock can find himself in wild social demand by all of even the most-A of A-Gays. As that great scholar of A-Gays, Sutherland, in the *magnum opus, Dancer from the Dance*, noted, there are "only two requirements for social success with those queens in the Hamptons (old money A-Gays): a perfect knowledge of French and a big dick." However, what A-Gays do not like are people with great wealth *and* great cocks. One or the other, dear— make up your mind. Some things are just *too* much; A-Gays are horrified by the ostentatious. And remember: if it is between money and anything else (except *more* money), money, as is its wont, wins.

A-Gays are very loyal to their own. Once you are an acknowledged A-Gay, you are one for life (unless you commit a truly reprehensible sacrilege, like going to three B-Gay parties in a row). This is the reason why most gatherings of A-Gays resemble geriatric wards. But A-Gays do love to try to recruit new members. Since they see each other constantly, they've got to do *something* to avoid boring each other to death. The portals to A-Gayhood are always open, but the guardians are stricter in their admission policies than the arbiters of what is and what is not correct attire at the a GMSMA meeting (which is, by the way, a favorite hang out of Fun Gays).

By Designation Only

One thing you must never do is *ask* for admission to A-Gayland. ("If you have to ask if you're ready, you are not," declares one A-Gay so high up on the social scale his nose bleeds constantly.) You must be found by other A-Gays. Some are born A, others achieve A-ness, and still others have A-ness thrust upon them. Born As include those gays from the very best A-Gay families (an A-Gay's third cousin, fresh out of Choate and ready to have Uncle Leslie—a very A-Gay name—show him The City [code for Manhattan below 96th St.] is almost automatically A); gays with a great deal of very old money, and gays who come into the world knowing Greta Garbo's phone number. Fun Gays generally must achieve A-ness: a Fun Gay on the verge of a percentage-of-the-gross (*not net*) contract with a major film studio or about to be cast in a lead part in a Hal Prince musical will be most seriously considered for entry into the ranks of A-Gays. Even a lowly B-Gay can have A-ness thrust upon him by, for example, simply moving into a highly desirable ten-room Park Avenue co-op. "In *that* building, darling, *everyone* is A" is how an A-Gay explains his wholehearted welcome of a former-B into A-Gay circles.

Except for some born A-Gays, there is a probationary period for all gays who have risen through the ranks. This period generally lasts for a dozen or so seasons. ("Season" is a favorite A-Gay word, used instead of "year;" for reasons too obvious to enumerate, A-Gays do not like to think about years.) During this time, the A-Gay on probation is relentlessly tested by tenured As. One little slip is all it takes to make you eternally an "almost A." Is that domestic wine you are serving? Tsk, tsk. A balcony seat at Carnegie Hall? Tsk, tsk. A house for the summer in *Cherry Grove?* Tsk, tsk. You *like Batman?* Tsk, tsk. Is that a *reproduction* on your wall? Tsk, tsk. But if you survive the inspection, there is good news: you can think (but never call) yourself an A-Gay. (A-Gays love false modesty: To speak too much of being A is very B.) And once you're a genuine A-Gay, you need not ever worry about being cast out of the group because of your ever-advancing age. Being an A-Gay means never having to say you're an old troll. (The Fun Gays aren't so lucky: a Fun Gay over 45 is a contradiction in terms.) Just look at all those ancient A-Gays wandering around Sutton Place. Like gargoyles on top of Notre Dame cathedral—ugly as hell, but very difficult to knock off.

How To Become An A-Gay

How do you become an A-Gay? There are no real rules because there are too many exceptions. But there are some general guidelines. There is no such thing as an A-Gay place to go dancing. Mars is "cute," M.K. "clever," The World "interesting"—but these are principally where Fun Gays take A-Gays. The Saint-at-large used to be very A-Gay for its first party, but it quickly became very "bridge and tunnel" (the A-Gay way of saying "the pits, Mary") and is now notorious for its B-Gays. If truth be known, most A-Gays are terrible dancers anyway who would prefer to refrain from humiliating themselves on dance floors *anywhere.*) Limelight is so far out now, it may soon become in again. Stay tuned. Strangely enough, Paddles still gets its share of slumming A-Gays—though, it goes without saying, an A-Gay never admits to going there.

Donating large amounts of money to worthy causes is not an automatic entree to A-Gayness, but contributions can't hurt. The only major organization in New York that means anything socially is the Metropolitan Opera Guild. The Gay Men's Health Crisis and the New York City Gay Men's Chorus are moderately fashionable, but it is very un-A to publicize—or even admit to—donations to these groups or, for that matter, to any group with the word "gay" in the title. (What *will* the bank think when it sees the check?) A-Gays are still quite closeted (or, as they say, "discreet"). It is extremely A-Gay to, like Gore Vidal, profess dislike of the use of the word "gay" as anything but a synonym for "happily excited." And it means social oblivion for an A-Gay to volunteer services of any kind to a gay organization or to march in the Gay Pride Parade. Some very adventurous A-Gays *watch* the parade, but traditional A-Gays—the vast majority—prefer to spend the last Sunday in June at the Pines, just as they've done since the fall of Constantinople.

A-Gays love to eat (which is why there are so many overweight—or, as they themselves put it, "healthy-looking"—A-Gays), and there are lots of A-Gay restaurants. But since these joints go in and out of favor with alarming frequency, it's difficult for a non-A to find one. But permanently out are Lutece, 21, and Elaine's, since A-Gays hyperventilate when they are in the company of people more snobbish than themselves. Also out are all restaurants where chopsticks are used in lieu of knives, forks and spoons. (A-Gays are very big on upholding tradition: if chopsticks were proper, Mumsy would have seen to it that they were used back in Grosse Point.) However, if you are served a mesquite-grilled chicken at a ridiculously inflated price or a pizza topped with kiwi and caviar, you are at least on the right track in your search for an A-Gay restaurant.

Laziness is a great sin for an A-Gay. A-Gays do not "hang out" unless it's in a cafe in Mykonos to rest between bouts of

A Brief Guide To What's A, What's Fun, What's B

A	FUN	B
Key West (in season)	Key West (out of season)	Fort Lauderdale
Smoked salmon	Dim-sum	Flavored popcorn
A kiss on the cheek	SM	Fucking and sucking
Anita O'Day	Diana Ross	Barbra Streisand
Brown leather	Black leather	Naugahyde
The Plaza	The Chelsea	Howard Johnson's
Backgammon	Trump	Poker
Rizzoli	A Different Light	B. Dalton
Movies on VCR	Movies in Theaters	Movies on VCR
Uncle Charlie's	The Spike	Ty's
A dear, dear friend	A hot trick	A lover
Golden Girls	*Golden Girls*	*Golden Girls*
Cocaine	MDA	Poppers
Edmund White	John Preston	Gordon Merrick
The New Yorker	*The Village Voice*	*The New Yorker*
Harvard	NYU	Community colleges
Mozart	Verdi	Wagner
"Delightful"	"Hot"	"Super"
Monte Carlo	Atlantic City	Las Vegas
LA Law	*Wiseguy*	*Roseanne*
Ralph Lauren	Levi's	Izod-Lacoste
PBS	HBO	ABC
Harry Reasoner	Mike Wallace	Diane Sawyer
Thanksgiving	Halloween	Valentine's Day
Imported champagne	Domestic champagne	Cold Duck
Greta Garbo	Bette Davis	Joan Crawford
Baccarat	Blackjack	Slot machines
Cezanne	Matisse	Picasso
Beatrice Lillie	Sandra Bernhard	Joan Rivers
Maria Callas	Marilyn Horne	Renata Scotto
Robert Redford	Clint Eastwood	Burt Reynolds
Beefeater martini	Budweiser	Lite
The Pines	The roof	Riis Park
Park Avenue	Central Park	Washington Square Pk
Limos	Bicycles	Taxis
"The Women"	Dykes	Lesbian people
Homosexuals	Fags	Gays
A Chorus Line	*A Chorus Line*	*Les Miserables*
Bloomingdale's	Macy's	Alexander's

shopping. A-Gays are always very busy ("There aren't enough hours in the day—I barely made it to the concert in time" is a classic A-Gay sentence): a minimum of twenty hours a week (more if possible) must be spent seriously shopping (shopping is A-Gay therapy; it is so comforting to know that no matter how much one has, there is always so much *more* to buy); three hours a week playing squash (or polo, if at all possible)—all other forms of exercise are currently non-A, exceptions being swimming in private pools and facial isometrics; and twenty-five hours a week of imbibing hard-core culture (opera, ballet, museums, flea markets, but not off-off Broadway—no matter *what* a Fun Gay tells you—and, above all, *absolutely* no rock concerts.)

The A-Gay Party

To be an A-Gay, you *must* give inventive parties. One of the reasons that there are so few A-Gays under 30 is that young gays think a great party consists of a lot of people, a lot of beer, and a lot of pot. The traditional A-Gay bash is a sit-down dinner for ten, but occasionally larger gatherings are called for. If you receive an invitation to a theme party—generally called something like A Night In India or A Tribute To Carmen Miranda or Christmas In July—you can be pretty sure that it's being given by an A-Gay. A number of guests at a "tremendous" [code to indicate to other As that Fun Gays and perhaps even B-Gays will very likely be present] A-Gay party are regulated by a strict formula: one Fun Gay for every eight or nine A-Gays. Sometimes, if the party is to be very large (over a hundred invitations), a few token B-Gays will be invited, since A-Gays like to pride themselves on how friendly they are. A-Gays are always saying, "I'm a people person," which translates as, "Not only do I know non-As, but my maid is a lovely black woman."

Though A-Gays are very incestuous socially, they are almost rabidly puritanical sexually. One thing you must never, ever, ever do *ever* is steal an A-Gay's lover (which an A-Gay calls his "dear, dear friend"—two "dears;" an A-Gay's merely one-dear friend is his mother—or his "partner" or, among terribly entrenched A-Gays, his "husband" or his "other half"). Just try and break up an A-Gay relationship and not only will you be banished forever from the company of A-Gays, but you may very well never be allowed on the island of Manhattan again. One little lick on a "married" A-Gay's dick and you'll regret the day you were born.

Most A-Gays are couple-oriented. But it is terribly difficult for a non-A to become an A by merely fucking an uncoupled A-Gay. Some A-Gays are quite randy in their wild youth, but they almost universally settle down with another A-Gay they "prepped" with. However, some A-Gays have a partiality for young and beautiful and well-hung illiterates chanced upon in Acapulco, St. Tropez, or The Ninth Circle. But such "protégés," who are listed in the address books of other A-Gays as "& Other," come and come and come and come and go with admirable speed and are *never*, repeat *never* considered to be A-Gays themselves.

A-Gay Sexuality

Actually, A-Gays are really much too busy to have much sex. Whenever you hear, "I never thought sex was all that important; it's a bit overrated—don't you think?" you are definitely in the presence of an A-Gay. Oversexed A-Gays do it once a week, but once a month is about average. (A-Gays are much too demure to scream out anything so vulgar as "I'm coming, I'm coming, oh God, I'm coming" and instead generally prefer to announce orgasms after the fact: "I think I just came.") A-Gays love to joke about kinky sex, but remember, to an A-Gay, "kinky" means "that which smears the bronzer." An A-Gay may have a roomful of sex toys ("I found this amazing store called—what was it?—oh yes, The Pleasure Chest, and I thought I'd buy a few little things;" note: no matter what an A-Gay buys—a queen-sized rack, a $20,000 stereo system, Australia—it is always called a "little thing"), but make no mistake about this: they are just for show. Put a pair of handcuffs on an A-Gay and he turns into just another screaming queen.

When you come right down to it, this sort of gay male society is all silly, meaningless, and pretentious, but it gives a lot of fags something to do. Trouble is, when all is said and done, the majority of Manhattan A-Gays are B-Gays in San Francisco.

—This essay could not have been written were it not for Rex Reed's pioneering study of A-ness, Fun-ness, and B-ness, "A Compleat Guide to the Hollywood Society Game," in People Are Crazy Here *(New York: Delacorte Press, 1974).*

8

REMAKING FILM CLASSICS WITH GAY CHARACTERS
The Trouble With Horny

The theatrical re-release of the five "lost" Hitchcock films—*Rear Window, Vertigo, The Trouble With Harry, Rope,* and the 1956 *Man Who Knew Too Much*—and Donald Spoto's excellent biography of Hitchcock, *The Dark Side of Genius,* have sparked a renewed interest in the cinema's quintessential master.

And now right here in this article, the last chapter (I swear) of the Hitchcock story will be revealed. Spoto told you all about Hitchcock's bathroom habits and what Janet Leigh said about Saul Bass's opinion of the fast-moving reverse shot of the knife entering the abdomen in the shower scene, but now I will tell you that four of Hitchcock's greatest films were originally in as all-gay productions! Yes, it's true! *Vertigo, The Birds, Notorious,* and *Psycho* were initially intended to be tales of homosexual life—as opposed to *Strangers On A Train* and *Rope* which wound up being stories about homosexual life despite the initial intentions. But social pressures compelled Hitchcock to remake the four gay films, straightening them out, so to speak.

But *I*, working ceaselessly in dusty archives and sleazy bars, have managed to unearth the original gay treatments for these four Hitchcock masterpieces, and I hereby present their plots and other hitherto unknown anecdotes for the first time in this essay.

Vertigo

James Stewart plays Scottie, a San Francisco detective, who discovers his morbid fear of discos when his "sister" (John Wayne) dies of an overdose of animal tranquilizers while staking out a dance joint suspected of admitting heterosexuals. Scottie's fear is manifested in vertigo, a psychosomatic illness that produces dizziness and a sensation of floating in space—sort of like what happens when reading the novels of David Leavitt.

Scottie then resigns from the police force and is asked by the owner of a gay gas station (Divine) to follow his lover (Jack Wrangler). Divine tells Scottie that Jack has become possessed by a long-dead relative (Oscar Wilde) who hopes to lure Jack into a leather bar to participate in a crucifixion scene. Nothing heavy. And Scottie seems to believe this, which is just one of the film's sublime mysteries.

The detective reluctantly accepts the job, figuring that maybe he'll be able to use it as a plot of a TV series, where the real money is, and trails Jack, eventually saving him when he attempts to enter the Mineshaft. But in spite of Scottie's desire to protect Jack from sordidness, Scottie cannot rescue Jack when Jack enters The Blessed and throws himself from the balcony to the dance floor when the D.J. refuses to play "I Am What I Am" one more time. Overwhelmed by guilt and the loss of the man he had come to love, Scottie suffers a breakdown that not even his drug dealer (Larry Hagman) can alleviate.

When he eventually gets better, Scottie sees a man whose striking resemblance to the dead Jack elicits a Pygmalion-like obsession in Scottie. Scottie follows this man and asks him to brunch at the Spike, even though he was supposed to protect the "first" Jack from such environments. Are you noticing inconsistencies? Well, who are *you* to criticize? This is great filmmaking. You want logic, go read Kant's *Prolegomena to Any Future Metaphysics* . . . which ain't a load of laughs, though Hitchcock was influenced by Kant while making *Vertigo*, particularly by the philosopher's views on hair-dos.

At this point, the most famous flashback in the history of movies occurs. Jack, it turns out, was not really Divine's lover, but just his fuck buddy, and a participant in a carefully contrived plot to kill the real lover by throwing him into a crowd of politically correct lesbians who had been spurred to murderous hatred by attending a lecture by Andrea Dworkin on pornography. Scottie, in reality or in "reality," has been set up as a witness to an apparent suicide that masked a murder. Or maybe it's the other way around.

Anyway, the flashback ends or maybe it doesn't and then there's a scene in which Scottie takes the "second" Jack to a leather boutique and has him try on chaps and, as a result, film students have never lacked for something to write about.

This transformation scene in the leather boutique has excited so much comment that I'm glad I can now present the scene exactly as originally written:

> *Stewart (selecting clothes for Wrangler): No, that's not it.*
>
> *Salesqueen: But you said basic black leather, Sir.*
>
> *Stewart: Now look, faggot—I just want an ordinary, simple pair of black leather chaps. No piss-elegant silver studs.*
>
> *Wrangler: I like the purple velvet chaps with the sequins.*
>
> *Stewart: Shut up, asshole. After this movie, you'll wind up owning a tacky guesthouse in Key West and writing a column for* Stallion *magazine and I'll be getting career achievement awards by the dozen and talking funny on Johnny Carson and getting to die with Bette Davis in an HBO movie. Critics for the next hundred years, maybe more, will be writing learned monographs on my performance in this film while you'll be forever known as the one who flawed this otherwise perfect Hitchcock movie.*
>
> *Salesqueen: Your Master is right, Jack.*
>
> *Stewart: I just want you to look hot, Jack. I know the kind of leather that will look good on you.*
>
> *Wrangler: No, I won't do it!*
>
> *Stewart: Don't push me, bitch! (to salesqueen) Now, I'd like to see a whip—long, black leather, with a heavy handle.*

Of course, full understanding of this scene depends on understanding the scene when Scottie first meets the "second"

Jack. Or is it when he has a second meeting with the "first" Jack? Here's the original of *that* scene:

> *Stewart: Will you let me tie you up?*
> *Wrangler: Tie me up and what else?*
> *Stewart: Just tie you up at first. Later we could get into watersports.*
> *Wrangler: Why? Just because I remind you of him? Or me? Or someone. What do I care anyway? I'm nothing but a piece of meat. That's not very complimentary. Don't you want to do anything else to me?*
> *Stewart: No.*
> *Wrangler: That's not very complimentary either.*
> *Stewart: I just want to tie you up.*
> *Wrangler: Alright, already! Maybe I should let Kim Novak take this part.*

So, when they've all got this stuff off their chests, the "second" Jack wears a dog collar that the "first" Jack used to wear and Scottie figures out the truth by forcing Jack back up the balcony of the Blessed where he is surprised by the sudden materialization of a film student doing a thesis on "Verisimilitude in the Acting of Jack Wrangler."

The Birds

A rich but boring faggot (John Travolta) meets a YAGUP— a young, aspiring gay urban professional (Tom Selleck) in a record store. Despite the YAGUP's rudeness (he refuses to do S/M with John, who seriously needs some discipline), John is attracted to him and goes to the YAGUP's house to deliver a rare, pirated Grace Jones concert tape. John then learns that the YAGUP lives with two highly amusing older homosexuals (Ronald Reagan and Jerry Falwell) for whom John leaves the cassette as a gift. Returning to town, John is annoyed by a cha-cha queen who claims to know the "real truth" about AIDS. Later, John accepts an invitation to the YAGUP's house for dinner, in spite of the fact that he knows that Ronald and Jerry have seen *Two of a Kind* and are out for John's blood.

Fear and loathing pervade the air. Obviously, something is very wrong with the cha-cha queens in the area—Diana Ross fans are seen associating with Donna Summer fans; one cha-cha is observed keeping a secret; a Hispanic cha-cha admits to really being from Puerto Rico. But John pays no notice and goes to the dinner. A group of mad cha-cha queens crash the dinner, torturing everyone by using the word "faaaabulous" at least once in every sentence.

The nastiness of the cha-chas increases. A flock of cha-chas force John to listen to stories about their acting careers. An innocent leatherman (Rod Taylor)—is badgered to death by cha-chas outraged because his drapes are "too busy and in last year's colors besides." The YAGUP's ex-lover (Cary Grant) is killed by a stampede of cha-chas racing to see Cher at the Sands. Finally, John, the YAGUP, Ron, and Jer are held prisoners by thousands and thousands of cha-chas at a cocktail party. After John is ruthlessly abused by savage cha-chas who "want to get to know the real you before we have sex," the YAGUP and his roommates decide that this nonsense has gone on much too long. After the cha-chas are all Quaaluded into stupors, the YAGUP and those two highly amusing older homosexuals, Ronnie and Jer-jer, take John to a library, hoping he'll eventually re-learn the art of watching TV without moving his lips.

Rarely has a performer had to put up with such abuse as Travolta did in the filming of *The Birds*, which was recast with Tippi Hedren mid-way into production. Travolta had been told, before the filming of the final attack of the cha-chas began, that of course mechanical cha-chas would be used, since to use real cha-chas would be too disgusting. But when Travolta arrived on the set one Monday to begin shooting, he was told that mechanical cha-chas would not be used because of objections raised by the powerful Cha-Cha Queens' Union.

A shocking new approach was then tried. The crew, wearing ear plugs and carrying huge cartons, were carefully positioned, facing the actor, who stood against a wall. The entire set was enclosed in a giant cage and then, as Travolta waved his arms, live cha-chas were thrown at him and he defended himself with wild, increasingly honest and unacted gestures of terror.

The trial went on into Tuesday and then into Wednesday. More camera setups, more swift shots, more Lacoste shirts, more designer jeans. According to Ronald Reagan,

> *Day after day after day for an entire week, the poor actor put up with that. He was alone in that caged room with the cha-chas coming at him, and with all the Lacostes and all the designer jeans and all the hairspray and all the headbands and all the Adidases. Why, the poor girl couldn't even smoke a joint in peace.*

On Thursday, Hitchcock discovered a new problem. Those shots in which Travolta was forced to the floor as the cha-chas continued to attempt to have "really, I mean, really, deep" conversations with him weren't realistic enough.

In an exclusive interview Travolta recalls, "And so on Thursday, the wardrobe mistress took me into my dressing room, where elastic bands were tied around my body, with nylon thread that was pulled through tiny holes in my costume. I soon found out what this was for. One leg of each cha-cha was tied to each piece of string, so that when I lay on the floor I couldn't get away from them."

On Friday, Thursday's ordeal was repeated for close shots and odd angles. Then one cha-cha queen became particularly agitated and started to talk about furniture. Travolta became hysterical and suffered a collapse, necessitating the substitution of Hedren.

Notorious

The original film version of *Notorious* was rejected by the studio not because it dealt with gay characters, but because, not content with being homosexuals, the leading characters insisted on being writers, as well. The head of the Catholic Legion of Decency spoke for millions when he said, "It's all well and good to make a movie about cocksuckers, but to make a movie about cocksuckers who are writers—well some things are just *too* much!"

In the interests of decorum, I will offer only a very brief outline of the original story of *Notorious*. A gay writer (T.R.

Witomski), son of a gay writer (W.H. Auden), is pressed by the Gay Press Association to outwit a group of very cheap publishers. Although in love with the gay writer who recruited him for this task (John Preston), T.R. actually agrees to have sex with a particularly unsavory gay editor (Truman Capote) who, in league with an evil literary agent (K.D. Bliss), forces him to write porno until he throws up. There's a classic scene in which T.R. walks out of an office putting a typewriter ribbon through his ears and then he finds a j/o story hidden in a bottle of poppers in the refrigerator which is supposed to resolve everything. And then the writers live happily ever after. Well, as happily as people can live when they are involved in such an ugly pasttime as writing.

Psycho

Hitchcock did something unique with the original *Psycho*: it was filmed in a gay bar in real time, thereby establishing a new standard for tedium.

Stopping at a bar for a refreshing cocktail Marlon Crane (Tom Cruise), who has just stolen a brilliant idea from his employer (Harvey Fierstein) of Designing Designs, Inc. meets Norman Bates (Anthony Perkins), a sensitive homosexual who is shunned by everyone because he lives in New Jersey. Norman offers to buy Marlon a cheese sandwich and a glass of milk, even though what Marlon really needs at this point is a triple vodka martini with a twist. But Marlon tries to be a lady about it and compliments Norman on the wonderful collection of stuffed birds he has hanging from his belt *on the right*. ("I wonder what *that* is supposed to mean?" Marlon thinks, making a mental note to read the articles in gay magazines that explain these things.)

Marlon then goes to the bathroom. The scene that follows is, of course, so famous that I would only insult the intelligence of readers to write about it any more.

Strangely enough, it was not the brutality of this scene that caused Paramount to insist that Hitchcock heterosexualize the film: it was the unprecedented shot of a gay man *not* wearing Levi 501s and admitting "Honestly, I don't even own a pair."

According to a studio memo Hitchcock was told that "Artistic license is one thing, Mary, but some things are just *too* much!"

Anyway, then all sorts of people run in and out of the bar bothering Norman. There's Marlon's roommate, Leon (Sean Penn). Leon and Marlon used to be lovers of a sort but it didn't really work out because Marlon just couldn't give up the baths and Leon couldn't bring himself to use such terms as "primary significant other but in the context of an open relationship" without giggling. And then there's Leon's third ex-lover's current lover once removed, Johan (Kevin Bacon), who's into painlessly killing insects. And then there's a hustler (Scott Baio) that Leon has hired.

It all gets pretty complicated now so pay attention because I don't want to hear anybody kvetching, "If it's so great, why doesn't it make sense?" Norman, it is learned, has been behaving very nastily: sometimes he plays top and sometimes he plays bottom. (And he keeps changing those damn stuffed birds from one side to another!) Leon says to Norman, "I heard my third ex-lover's current lover once removed fucked you. Can I fuck you too?" And Norman say, "I don't get fucked." Then Johan says to Norman, "I heard you fucked your roommate even though you couldn't bring yourself to give up the baths and he, well, never mind, but will you fuck me?" And Norman says, "I don't fuck." Then the hustler tries to make sense out of all this and dies of confusion.

Okay, then a psychiatrist (Cary Grant) appears, and he comes to the brilliant conclusion that Leon and Johan should just go have sex together and leave Norman alone. Finally, Norman gives his great final speech:

> *I can't do anything but stand here and stare, like one of these goddamned stuffed birds I'm carrying around with me. Why am I doing that? I must read those articles in the gay magazines that explain these things. All these numbers in this bar know I can't even say "Hello" or I'll be accused of being desperate. And everybody hates desperate queens. So I'll just stand here in case they do think I'd like to get laid once in a while without going through all this top and bottom*

bullshit. They're probably watching me—well, let them. They'll see what kind of person I am. I'm not even going to cruise that number. The one with all those muscles. I hope they are all watching. They'll see and they'll know and they'll say, "Why she wouldn't even cruise that number. The one with all the muscles."

9

How to Seduce
A Heterosexual

Yes, it's true. There is an army of millions of homosexuals out there working ceaselessly day and night to seduce innocent heterosexuals. Though these evil homosexuals (is there any other kind?) employ many and varied methods to achieve their nefarious purpose, a typical such seduction scenario takes place in an ordinary tavern, just like the one in your lovely neighborhood.

At this establishment, typically called "The Dew Drop Inn" or another equally charming name, a group of mild-mannered heterosexual gentlemen are demurely sitting at the bar, tastefully sipping refreshing beverages and discussing current events such as "those fuckin' Yankees," "my fuckin' foreman," "my fuckin' wife," "my fuckin' kids," and "fuckin'." Unbeknownst to them, a vicious faggot has entered the bar with a shocking goal in his perverted mind: he will attempt to gain unlawful access to a penis belonging to one of the saintly heterosexual gentlemen present.

Homosexuals, it is well known, are masters of disguise. Seemingly without effort, even the most predatory homosexuals are able to affect the appearance of "looking just like everyone else." Yes, for all you know, a homosexual may be sitting next to you *right now*. Since homosexuals have been taught to blend in well with their surroundings, it is impossible in most instances to know for sure who is a fine, understanding heterosexual (is there any other kind?) and who is a despicable homosexual up to no good.

Just as the appearance of homosexuals can be deceiving, so can their conversation. Homosexuals have all taken special classes in which they have learned to talk about *the very same things* that normal people talk about. Many homosexuals can discuss the weather, politics, and sports. The person who says to you "Hot, ain't it?" or "Think Ollie will go to jail?" or "Whaddya think of them Tigers?" may actually be a homosexual with designs on your pristine heterosexual body.

Meanwhile, back at the Dew Drop Inn, a shocking scene is in process. The homosexual interloper has cornered his heterosexual prey. Though the pure-at-heart (and very religious) heterosexual does not know it yet, he is about to fall victim to a savage, merciless attack from the homosexual. The fact that the heterosexual is 6' 5" and weighs 250 lbs. while the homosexual is 5' 7" and weighs 140 lbs. matters not at all. Homosexuals are agile, wily, and treacherous. Once a homosexual has singled out a heterosexual as the object of his indecent attentions, that heterosexual is powerless. Many people believe that homosexuals are in league with the Devil. That is true.

Homosexuals will stop at nothing to seduce heterosexuals. As everyone knows, heterosexual sexual relations occur only for the procreation of children in the sanctity of marriage and are squarely based in the mutual love and respect of the partners involved, while homosexual sexual relations are only attempts to satisfy the basest type of sub-animal lust. Right now at the Dew Drop Inn, the homosexual is forcing the heterosexual to consume vast quantities of alcoholic beverages. (Such a scene has never been known to happen when a heterosexual man encounters a heterosexual woman at a tavern; they will merely discuss how much they each love Jesus, praise the Lord together for a few moments, and then part company.) Sometimes, the homosexual will even threaten the heterosexual: "Ready for another one?"

Since the heterosexual is beginning to fear for his very life, he will often permit the homosexual to buy him "another one."

After a sufficient number of "another ones," the heterosexual is in a weakened condition and is quite vulnerable to the next onslaught by the homosexual. (Heterosexuals rarely have more than one or two drinks in the course of an evening, while all homosexuals drink like fishes and will not allow heterosexuals to drink their beverage of choice—lo-cal, caffeine-free cola—in their company.)

Once the homosexual has the heterosexual under the influence of demon alcohol, the lawless homosexual often orders the law-abiding heterosexual to consume, most often by smoking or sniffing, dangerous and illegal drugs, which the heterosexual has, needless to say, never encountered before. Or even heard of, for that matter. Sometimes this drug abuse occurs in the homosexual's vehicle, sometimes even at the homosexual's place of residence. (Homosexuals live in houses and apartments just like real people; some homosexuals even own cars, too.)

How does the homosexual get the heterosexual to accompany the homosexual to the homosexual's vehicle or place of residence? By more mind-boggling threats: "Wanna get high?" or "Smoke a joint?" The poor, scared heterosexual believes that if he "humors" the marijuana-wielding homosexual, the homosexual will leave him alone. The heterosexual has no way of knowing, naturally, that after he uses these drugs against his will, the homosexual will insist on *other things*.

Once the heterosexual is alone with the homosexual, all vestiges of sanity, morality, and common decency are lost. Nancy Reagan was so on-target when she told the *National Enquirer* that all homosexuals should be forced by federal law to have signs on their front (and back) doors that read "Abandon hope all ye who enter here."

Since this is a decent family publication, I will not go into too much detail about exactly what the homosexual does to the heterosexual at this stage of the seduction. It is *very* disgusting, particularly because the innocent heterosexual is unable to resist the trap that has been set by the homosexual. The best the heterosexual can do under these circumstances is to close his eyes tightly, think of the future of England, and wait for the homosexual to finish. Then the homosexual will usually release the now-drained and debilitated heterosexual, though sometimes the homosexual humiliates the heterosexual even further by taunting him in a secret language known only to faggots: "You're a hot man. Maybe we can do this again sometimes."

As if all this were not horrible enough, I have even more shocking news to convey. I shall attempt not to be too raunchy here, but we must all realize that the truth is ofttimes ugly, and it is the writer's sacred duty to report the truth no matter how terrible it is. While nothing would give me more pleasure than to shield my delicate heterosexual readers from the full and exact nature of the homosexual threat, I feel that only if we know our enemies can we conquer them.

The sick fact is that homosexuals have mastered certain vile sexual techniques, the exact nature of which I will, of course, not commit to print; some homosexuals are even self-admitted "experts" in these crude practices. But the real tragedy is that these unconscionable acts of grotesque lust feel quite good to some naive heterosexuals when they are performed on them by these sinful homosexuals. Some heterosexuals have been known to say "Wow! That feels great!" or "Oh yeah, man, do it, do it, do it good" while they are under the spell of homosexuals. It is not even unknown for a heterosexual to (mistakenly, of course) opine while involved against his will in one of these unspeakable acts "You do that much better than my wife." Of course, no matter what the heterosexual says, he doesn't really mean it. The heterosexual is completely blameless; the nasty homosexual has *made* him say these things. The heterosexual is merely the victim of the homoerotic Communist conspiracy. All heterosexuals must remember one cardinal rule: "If it feels good, don't let it be done to you."

I have so far restricted my discussion of the homosexual menace to male homosexuals who seduce male heterosexuals, but I would be remiss in my solemn duties as a journalist if I did not at least briefly address another insidious aspect of the homosexual plot to destroy American life as we know it. Though research in this area is spotty (for most people cannot believe such dementia even exists), unimpeachable sources maintain that in addition to the evil male homosexuals out there, there are also evil female homosexuals out there. The female homosexuals are called "lesbians" because they are all born on the Greek island of Lesbos. And these female homosexuals are just as savage and just as without redeeming social value in their seduction of innocent female heterosexuals as their male counterparts are in the seduction of innocent male heterosexuals.

Think of the tremendously dreadful ramifications of this revelation. While innocent male heterosexuals are being trapped into unspeakable acts of sexual outrage by male homosexuals, their innocent wives and innocent girlfriends and innocent sisters and innocent mothers are being trapped into participating in similar (but anatomically different) acts of sexual outrage by female homosexuals. No one is safe; homosexuals are after everyone.

What is to be done? We are obviously faced with a serious problem of massive proportions. The solution must be, of necessity, drastic: heterosexuals are simply going to have to stop going out in public. Homosexuals have been known to attack heterosexuals on beaches, in the supermarket, on public transportation, in bathrooms on the interstate and in state and county parks, in shopping malls, even on quiet, tree-lined streets in residential heterosexual communities. In fact, everywhere. No place is safe since homosexuals are able to freely roam anywhere they choose to. There are homosexuals in movie theaters, homosexuals on golf courses, homosexuals in restaurants. You can go out to buy a simple six-pack of non-alcoholic beer and run into a homosexual at the liquor store. You can go to a PTA meeting and meet a homosexual there. You can go to a gas station and encounter a homosexual. One course of action—and only one course—is open to heterosexuals who wish to safeguard themselves from contact with the disease of homosexuality: *stay home!*

But staying home is only part of the solution. Once all you decent heterosexuals have resolved never to leave your places of residence again, you must also resolve never to let anyone *into* your places of residence again. Homosexuals are unbelievably crafty. If you do not (pardon the expression) come to them, they will come to you. To save yourselves from unwanted homosexual advances, you heterosexuals must never open your doors. After all, you don't know who may be there. It could be a homosexual encyclopedia salesperson, a homosexual who works for AT&T, a homosexual who says he/she merely wishes to "read your meter," which is a homosexual slang term that roughly translates as "do a nasty on your body." Don't listen to them. Homosexuals may *say* they are seeking admission to your house to put the fire out in your living room and save your children from being burned to cinders, but all homosexuals have only one reason for visiting you: they wish to gain familiarity with your "naughty bits."

And when I tell you to admit no one into your homes, I mean *no one*. Not one person. Not nobody. People will come to you with a wide variety of seemingly plausible reasons why you should admit them into your homes: "I'm your father," "I'm your brother," "I'm your son." Under no circumstances let these people in. *Anyone* could be a homosexual; the dearest member of your family could force you to read *Drummer* and thus damn you forever to a life of unrepentant homosexuality. Consider everyone to be a potential homosexual and you'll have a fighting chance to maintain your heterosexual purity.

I realize that this article appears to be both shocking and fatalistic. But while it is true that homosexuals are gaining on the heterosexuals and hope is steadily waning, I do have some hopeful words to impart to you before I leave you to continue to fight the good fight against homosexuality.

There are some very heroic men and women who have willingly taken on a very dangerous mission. These men and women are thoroughly heterosexual, but they are generally to be found in the company of homosexuals. Let Cynthia M. explain:

"I am a heterosexual female person, though you wouldn't know it to look at me. Realizing as I do the vast extent of the unscrupulous homosexual menace, I have devoted my life to remedying this situation. Much as I despise homosexuals (as all right-thinking people do), God has told me to go hang out in their company. He actually said, 'Go ye and hang out with my fruits.' I consider myself to be on a sacred crusade. Sacred crusades are very hard work and I must work long hours. As the prophet Faghagia said, 'She who knows a fruit is blessed in my eyes and will receive good seats at the next Liza Minnelli concert.' My self-appointed task is very difficult, but on those few occasions when I have been successful, I was able to say with great pride, 'That's one giant penis for Cynthia; one small step for heterosexuality.' "

10

An Open Letter to the Organizers of Next Year's New York Gay and Lesbian Pride Day

Dear People,

I'm not getting any younger, you know, and unless next year's parade is much different from this year's I'm afraid that on the last Sunday of June you'll find my dead body somewhere between 27th and 28th Streets. There are many aspects about the parade that need changing. Don't try to think of them because I'm going to tell you what they are:

❖ The date. Really now, just because our founding homosexuals thought the last week in June perfect for throwing a mass hissy fit in 1969, there is no reason we have to celebrate the anniversary of The Sacred Throwing Of A Parking Meter Through The Window Of The Blessed Stonewall Bar on the last week of June. It's *hot* in June. Remember you are not asking us just to get together and stand around being gay. You are asking us to walk a great distance, preferably while wearing attire that fully expresses our particular individual form of gayness. Why not hold the parade in April or September on a nice, cool day? Every leatherman, drag queen, and dyke on combat patrol will thank you. The last Sunday in June should be spent on the beach.

❖ The time. Haven't you people ever heard of Gay Standard Time? What *is* this noon starting time business? Are you folks *sure* you are really gay? You'd get twice as many people if you *said* the party was starting at noon, but if you held, deep in your hearts, no intention of doing anything before 3 p.m. The parade has already passed by when sensible homosexuals are just awakening. I'm baffled—do you really expect the typical homosexual who has been out dancing until 7:30 a.m. to show up *anywhere* at noon? Get serious. Start at 3 p.m.; finish at 5 p.m., just in time for cocktails. Be civilized, damnit!

❖ The length. Fuck this sixty, seventy blocks shit. It's okay for those of you who have been spending all your free time for the past year making nuisances of yourselves in gyms and annoying the muggers by running around the Central Park Reservoir, but it's hell on earth for the rest of us. What's wrong with ten blocks? Is it carved in stone somewhere that "Verily, I say to ye, once a year, ye faggots and ye dykes shall walk until ye feet are numb to show ye gayness"? It is not. I can be just as gay walking ten blocks as I can be walking seventy. More so, actually. Homosexuals forced to walk long, tedious miles become cross. They fight with their lovers. ("*You* wanted to march; *I* wanted to go to the Pines.") The genders kvetch about each other. ("The dykes always get to go first." "The faggots really come out of the woodwork for this.") Dire imprecations are called down on the heads of whoever thought this all up in the first place. And these cross homosexuals are not going to appear nice and gay for the TV cameras. Image, darling, image! Cross homosexuals are not going to write large gay checks for worthy gay causes. Money, darlings, money! Cross homosexuals are not going to say, "Oh how gay. We must be sure, Roger or Beverly, to come all the way from Erie, Pennsylvania again next year." No. Cross homosexuals are going to publish nasty open letters.

❖ The speeches. Now you are really going too far. It's bad enough that you force all these divine gay men and all these divine gay women to walk for countless hours, but then when they all get to where they are going, you punish them with long, tedious speeches. Are you all card-carrying sadists or what? (That is not a put-down, merely a query.) Darlings, for the love of Gertrude Stein, after their trek, the marchers need liquid refreshment, particularly of an alcoholic nature. They do not need a lecture by the vice-president of the Gay Students League of Tacoma, Washington on "The Beauty of Being Gay." No one who walks himself or herself into a virtual coma feels very beautiful anyway. No one feels very gay either. Besides, no one has ever given a good speech at a Gay Pride Rally. All the speeches boil down to "I'm gay, you're gay, we're all gay." We know *that* already or we wouldn't be here in the first place.

While I have you here, I'd like to address a few other issues.

Remember how this whole gay pride business started? Perhaps you are not students of history, so let me tell you. Once upon a time a very wise male homosexual teamed up with an equally wise female homosexual. They agreed each was as gay as the other and they said, "Let us spend a day being proud that we are gay and thus saved from a life devoted to reading *Playboy* and *Cosmopolitan*." And so was Gay Pride *Day* born.

But then dissenters arose and spoke: "It is not enough to devote one day a year to the commemoration of being proud we are gay. We must have a weekend, particularly a Saturday evening, for this noble purpose." (The fact that these dissenters were all owners of urban businesses that catered principally to homosexuals had, of course, nothing to do with their views.) So Gay Pride *Weekend* was born.

But then fund-raisers came from the most distant reaches of Chelsea and said, "A Gay Pride Weekend is not enough. On Saturday everyone hits the bars and commits unspeakable acts. On Sunday everyone atones. What time is left to us fund-raisers who wish to have brunch to benefit The Third World Lesbian Women's Save The Whales Society, a lunch for the S/Mers For Koch, a cocktail party for the Radical Gay Street Queens Unable To Afford Good Drag, a dinner for The Virginia Woolf Poetry and Four-Wheel Drive Club, and a dance of the Bisexual Quadriplegic National organization? We need a Gay Pride *Week*."

Perhaps perky twenty-year-old homosexuals can be gay, gay, gay for an entire week. *I cannot.* I'm just not *that* gay anymore. Don't get me wrong. I'm just as gay as anyone else, but between heavy bouts of being actively (or for that matter, passively) gay, I need to rest. At my age being too gay for too long upsets my ulcers. (You write for gay publications for as long as I have and you'll have ulcers too.) No way in hell can I be gay, gay, gay, gay, gay, gay, gay for an entire fuckin' week. If I get overtired from too much gaiety, I begin to hallucinate and see Harvey Fierstein *everywhere*. Let's go back to Gay Pride *Day*. It was fun. We could be simply gay with people we were not sleeping with. It was nice. We didn't have to overdose on Alice B. Toklas's brownies or go deaf from Cris Williamson tapes just because we knew, liked, and admitted that same-gender sex was a hell of a lot of fun.

What brilliant mind decides what order the various groups in the parade march in? Next year, don't let this person make this decision while on *those* drugs. Try new drugs. Try anything. But let's face it: the gay community is extremely diverse. It is not the best of ideas to have the Lesbian Atheists marching in close proximity to the Cocksuckers For Christ. And I have it on excellent authority that the Asexual League of America and the Anytime Anyplace With Anyone Motorcycle Club of Kew Gardens would prefer not to know each other. It is all well and good to preach gay unity, but compelling the B'nai Gay Synagogue to share a city block with the Gay Fourth Reich Movement passes from unity to stupidity rather quickly.

Now I am going to ask you to decide once and for all eternity whether we are going to march *uptown* or *downtown*. You—and you know who are—keep changing your minds about this. It's disgruntling to those homosexuals to find themselves being gay downtown when everyone who's anyone is being gay uptown. And the other way around. And when his decision is made, it is your solemn duty to publicize it—by which I don't mean just putting up cute little signs in bars decorated as corrals in the meat-packing district of Manhattan and making a tasteful announcement at a meeting of the Absolutely Positively Perfectly Politically Correct Lesbian Club of New Brunswick, New Jersey.

Speaking of lesbians, I adore them, of course. It is both refreshing and comforting to know that in a gathering of homosexuals some people will know how to change a flat tire. But for years I thought that lesbians were gay, just like me.

(Well, maybe not *just* like me, but more or less like me.) Now though, it appears that lesbians are not gay, they are lesbians, which was never in any doubt. But it's all becoming a grammatical mess. You can't easily use the word gay these days without adding "and lesbian" immediately following it. Thus the Gay Press Association is now The Gay and Lesbian Press Association, and Gay Pride Week is Gay and Lesbian Pride Week. This is silly. And must stop. Right now. Or else I fear one day we will be marching in the Gay and Lesbian and S/M and Cross-Dressers and Bisexual and Homosexual and Homophile and Just Plain Queer Parade. This is unwieldy and will look cramped on a button.

Well, I think that's about it. If I think of anything else, I'll let you know. Let's get busy. Busy, busy, busy.

Yours sincerely,
—*T.R. Witomski*

11

LITERARY COMMENTARY
ON *VICIOUS GOSSIP*

Mr. T(heophilus) R(oderick) Woisme is, of course, the famous gay writer. Of his works, *Cute Shoes, Slow Nights at the Baths and Other Tragedies of Modern Life, Transsexual Enema Nurse,* and the Scatfreak tetralogy are, very likely, the most respected.

Every year on August 8th, Mr. Woisme begins writing his "serious book—the big one, the one they've all been waiting for." Months ago he chose the title from a long list of them he keeps as a bookmark between pages 16 and 17 of the sixth Grove Press paperback printing of *Story of O.* On the afternoon of the 7th he is alarmed because he has not yet thought of a plot to which *Vicious Gossip* might apply.

Mr. Woisme is awakened by the ringing of the telephone. On the phone is an irate lesbian screaming. This suggests to Mr. Woisme that he begin *Vicious Gossip* with an irate lesbian screaming. On paper, though—praised be Jesus—not in actuality, she screams all afternoon, over and over again, in all possible ways, and only now, at dusk, is she screaming satisfactorily. Mr. Woisme can only write barefoot and facing west with a window on his left side. He does not know why.

Several weeks later, Mr. Woisme thinks deeply about a bit that ought to go into Chapter 3. But where? How can he inject a totally meaningless anecdote about Octavian swimming the

Channel while the other characters are desperately worrying about whether Hildegard murdered the dwarf gynecologist?

Mr. Woisme is easily distracted. When not actually writing down a sentence, he is found wandering about his hovel, picking up and putting down small tricks. He frequently hums, more in sorrow than in anger, Patricio's theme from Hubert's *Johan Embron*.

It is one of Mr. Woisme's better days. He writes so much that when he stops he is quite ill. After restoring himself with sauerkraut, he rereads *Vicious Gossip* as far as he has gotten with it. He smiles to himself, believing that Harold's reconciliation with Rebecca and subsequent death from AIDS is one of his better ideas.

Mr. Woisme finishes Chapter 9, and he now *must* decide where the plot is going and what will happen to it when it gets there. He wishes that he had not killed off the dwarf gynecologist, who would have been most useful in revealing the truth about Gregory at the end of Chapter 18. At the moment, no one else in the novel knows the truth about Gregory.

Out for a walk, Mr. Woisme stops near the toxic waste dump. A peculiar smell—a combination of orchids and artichokes—reaches his nostrils. He jots down a few notes he suspects may be needed when the action of *Vicious Gossip* shifts to Anton's apartment in Chelsea.

Mr. Woisme is almost asleep when his mind flashes on the perfect epigraph for *Vicious Gossip*: "She can't (something-or-other) so she talks." His mind's eye sees those words near the the bottom of the right-side page of an old magazine. If he finds the magazine, he will be most vexed if he discovers that he himself is the author of the quote.

After journeying to Montoloking Heights in search of a tape of *Dirty Adult Babies,* a video he has been talked into reviewing by the friend of an ex-lover of the editor of an obscure newsletter, Mr. Woisme's attention is captured by a bin of second-hand porno novels. He comes across a copy of *Frat House Orgy*, his thirty-third novel, and finds he had autographed it: "For Xavier—may Bangkok be forever!" Bangkok? Xavier?

The first draft of *Vicious Gossip* is more than half finished. But, problematically, for the last several days, its characters have been becoming a tad too real. Last night a minor character named Micah showed up at dinner. Mr. Woisme had been aware of Micah's passion for leather, but had not known that he used mustard on his french fries.

Mr. Woisme is skimming through the early chapters of *Vicious Gossip*, which he has not looked at in a very long time, and now he sees *Vicious Gossip* for what it is: dreck. He thinks himself mad for continuing to work on such grotesque drivel. Why didn't he become a spy? He will burn the ms. Why is there no fireplace? What is he doing in the gazebo with the ducks?

Even more frightening than writing the first chapters are writing the last. The characters are boring Mr. Woisme to tears. The plot has grown into a huge monster with dangling tentacles. He has lost the ability to summon up verbs and has just constructed a sentence consisting solely of seventeen adjectives. Furthermore, he has insomnia. Even reading *Black Joystick* (his fifty-first novel) does not induce sleep. In the light of dawn, he realizes his carpet is out to get him.

Though *Vicious Gossip* is almost finished, Mr. Woisme feels it is his community duty to attend a performance of Mascarellioni's *Chechia Ortlebia*, which is being done, for the first time since 1763 by the Stonewall Friends of Neglected Operas. Unfortunately, Mr. Woisme cannot even figure out one of the opera's twelve plots since his mind is on *Vicious Gossip*.

Mr. Woisme writes the last sentence of *Vicious Gossip*. His calmness and the tidiness of the room are deceptive. The ms. is stuffed into the file cabinet—between "Mineshaft" and "Muziak, Fred" (editor of the *North Dakota Gay and Lesbian Blade*) and Mr. Woisme is distraught. He has no feeling in his legs, tiny explosions are erupting in the back of his head, and his beard is falling off.

The next day, Mr. Woisme is barely conscious. He aimlessly lollygags around the hovel, leaving half-filled coffee cups and half-eaten bananas everywhere. From time to time he thinks about getting dressed. He dismisses the notion as being unduly vigorous. Nineteen days pass.

LITERARY COMMENTARY ON *VICIOUS GOSSIP*

Sometime later, with a case of cheap vodka nearby, Mr. Woisme begins to revise *Vicious Gossip*. Rewriting is even worse than writing. Not only does he have to think of new things, but he is forced to remember the old things. Before Mr. Woisme is finished, two-thirds of the ms. will have no resemblance to the original version. Among many other changes, the dwarf gynecologist has found the hidden room in Quentin's castle.

Holding *Vicious Gossip* not very neatly done up in aluminum foil, Mr. Woisme arrives at the office of his publishers, Sakkcloth and Ashes. He is, naturally, deathly afraid of elevators, but today the stairs look menacing too. The entire enterprise suddenly strikes him as being very stupid and he thinks he will simply drop the ms. into the river and save a lot of people a lot of problems.

Mr. Woisme escapes from Messrs. Sakkcloth and Ashes, who were most anxious to go into all the intricacies of a scheme to heterosexualize all of Mr. Woisme's work, and goes to call on a dear, dear friend, who is too busy to see him.

Before returning home, Mr. Woisme allows himself to be taken to a literary party held in the private room of La Escribitore Idiotica. Among his fellow authors, few of whom he recognizes and none of whom he knows or wishes to know are Edblack, Morddred, Haldeberstadant, Cottilian, Dwinkin, and Averett. The conversation deals exclusively with disappointing sales, inadequate publicity, worse than inadequate payments, libelous reviews, others' declining abilities, and the unspeakable torment of writing, of which everyone speaks much of.

Vicious Gossip is over, but not finished. The galleys arrive and Mr. Woisme cannot contain his disgust. At first he believes that Sakkcloth and Ashes have sent him someone else's novel. Later he faces the ugly reality and has to weigh whether it is more important not to come off sounding like a nerd *or* to keep strictly within the permitted number off AAs.

Mr. Woisme receives the sketch for the cover of *Vicious Gossip*. He can't believe it. Just exactly what drugs are Sakkcloth and Ashes on? Mr. Woisme wonders. The cover is totally valueless and tasteless, too. Also, his name is barely visible. Mr. Woisme looks forward to an exhilarating few hours explaining these sentiments to Sakkcloth and Ashes.

KVETCH

84

The ten free copies of *Vicious Gossip* arrive. There are forty people who expect to receive one of them. Mr. Woisme cannot afford to buy the thirty additional copies, which is good in a way because if he gave everyone who wanted one a free copy, no one would feel special and he'd get a lot of little notes of thanks ending with the remark that *Vicious Gossip* seems a tad down from your usual level but you probably needed the money real fast.

Mr. Woisme goes to the West Village to do some errands. He has been uncharacteristically thorough, and so it is late afternoon before he stops into a bookstore. Having made certain that *Vicious Gossip* is there, he spends a pointless half-hour studying the titles of other books.

Sakkcloth and Ashes thoughtfully send Mr. Woisme the reviews of *Vicious Gossip,* a very large heap due in no small part to Mr. Woisme's nasty habit of reviewing the books of others. Before reading the notices, Mr. Woisme prioritizes: he will first finish reading *Noteworthy Gay and Lesbian Martyrs of the Eleventh Century* which he began in 1947 only to bog down on page 42.

At a gathering held vaguely in his honor, Mr. Woisme is having a pleasant enough time until Dr. Garibaldo demands to know just what Mr. Woisme was getting at in Chapter 14. Mr. Woisme has no idea what Dr. Garibaldo is talking about. The confrontation goes on for many hours and eventually results in Mr. Woisme begging schoolchildren for Valium.

Standing in an unsavory bar, Mr. Woisme finds words going through his mind: whetstone, foreshadow, gutta-percha, opaque, subcortical, towhead, purbline, elegit, curdle, whereabouts, polycystic, cyclopropane, bysinosis, betimes, maltreat. . . .

12

"UNSAFE" PORNO
The New Gay Neo-Moralists

Recently, the editor of a gay sex magazine sent a story to an artist for illustrating. The artist replied, "I will have to decline to illustrate it. I realize that it's only fantasy, but even a man who draws cocks wrapped in barbed wire has limits and this reaches mine. I don't want to appear to condone with my contribution sex practices which go so clearly against current health needs."

Any freelancer certainly has the right to refuse any assignment for any reason. But at this financial level it's not something freelancers do very often. And when a freelancer does refuse an assignment, he or she generally offers a reason along the lines of "no *new* bondage and discipline until you pay for the *old* bondage and discipline" or simply "I'm too busy right now." But in this case the illustrator declined to do a drawing for a very explicit political reason: he did not want to "appear to condone" "unsafe" sex.

(Everyone knows that there is "unsafe" sex, but nobody is precisely sure what *exactly* it is. It depends on which guideline you believe. Though all the guides agree that ingesting semen orally or rectally and oral-anal contact are "unsafe,"* there's a

---

*True when this article was first written, but now there is some debate about oral sex even with ejaculation.

difference of opinion about the safety of fellatio and anal intercourse without ejaculation and deep kissing. Sexual practices that interest only a minority of gay men—watersports, scat, and fisting—are resoundingly branded "unsafe" though some variations on these acts may actually be quite safe. A key term in many of the "safe" sex guides—"the exchange of bodily fluids"—is quite vague: submit that bit to a bunch of tax lawyers and you'll come up with everything from mutual masturbation to sneezing on your lover.)

The Reactionary Current

What a concerned, health-conscious member of the gay community the artist must be. But on reflection, the illustrator's apparent nobility masks a disturbing reactionary current that is appearing with alarming frequency in the gay press. AIDS *is* causing an anti-gay backlash, and this backlash is being led by gay people themselves. Male homosexuals are becoming terrified of their own sexuality, and some gays are beginning to work against themselves under the guise of the "long-run good."

It is important to realize that the magazine in question here has been around a while and pre-dates the health crisis. The story that pushed past the artist's "limits" (entitled "A Taste of Cum") is in no way out of line with the material the magazine has always been publishing: it's a typical story—I've written hundreds of comparable tales, but not "A Taste of Cum." And the artist has illustrated similar stories before. The only variable here is the spectre of AIDS.

The fact that "A Taste of Cum" is pornographic shouldn't—but does—cloud the issue that the expression of homosexuality in words and pictures is coming under renewed scrutiny and that censorship of such material is very much in the air. My argument doesn't center on whether a particular sex act is "safe" or "unsafe" but on whether a depiction of a sex act labelled by someone-or-other as "unsafe" should be publishable. Porno, by its nature, has always been an easy target for "moralists" (now joined by those curious gay neo-moralists) because porno is designed to bring out strong responses in its readers and viewers. (A hard-on is a strong response to words and/or images, certainly stronger than the responses typically generated by, say, the material in *The New Yorker.*) It is impossible to write about porno without either praising or condemning it. And you can't be wishy-washy about your view (none of this "I like *some* of it" business) because, as Susan Sontag has written, "assessment of pornography is held firmly within the limits of the discourse employed by psychologists, professional moralists, and social critics. Pornography is . . . an occasion for judgment. It's something one is for or against. And taking sides about pornography is hardly like being for or against aleatoric music or Pop Art, but quite a bit like being for or against legalized abortion or federal aid to parochial schools."

The Present Danger

The prevailing neo-conservative ideology in this country and the renewed assault on porno are not unrelated. (You can date both from 1981 with the first inauguration of Reagan and the publication of Andrea Dworkin's *Pornography: Men Possessing Women.*) Reaganistic crypto-fascism likes easy targets; any reactionary system needs "good" enemies to keep it oiled, enemies that can be quickly "identified," if not always defined: "I know one when I see one." The favorite enemies of the present Administration include Communists, pro-choice advocates, and pornographers. (Rabid conservatives think all three are the same anyway—and probably Jewish as well.)

But pornography is basically only a literary and pictorial genre. A work of porno should be discussed as if one were discussing a work of science fiction or a Post-Impressionist painting, not as if one were discussing a nuclear arms treaty or closing the baths.

When something is particularly frightening, popular thought demands a scapegoat. This connection (fear=scapegoat) has been unchanged for thousands of years. If the weather was really lousy, the ancient Greeks found an Iphegenia to sacrifice. If a country's economics were fucked up, one group of people— generally Jews (though witches and sodomites did their time in pogroms, too)—were held responsible. Today, the budgetary woes are blamed on the poor, and politically correct gays are finding dat ol' devil porno is a good scapegoat for their fear of AIDS.

Porno and Disease

The idea that porno causes disease is not new. The Victorians worried a great deal about porno falling into the hands of innocent, unsuspecting people (women, children, and all members of the working class) who would presumably be so taken with the stuff that they'd rush out and fuck around until they died of syphilis. (Before penicillin, syphilis was as feared as AIDS is today—you got it from sex and it killed you.) Yet Victorian porno flourished; the depraved souls who supported the Victorian smut industry don't appear to have gotten more depraved as a result, and syphilis doesn't appear to have attacked readers of *The Pearl* and *The Exquisite* more frequently than it did non-readers of these publications, the *Playboy* and *Penthouse* of their day. (If what could give you syphilis had been considered "unsafe" sex, Victorian erotica was *unsafe*.)

Porno was believed to encourage people to have sex, and if pornographic material features "unsafe" practices, porno is therefore thought by the misguided to be encouraging people to risk getting AIDS. But most people I know don't need porno to encourage them to have sex. In fact, porno functions more as a sex substitute than as an order to "Go ye and do likewise." Most regular readers and viewers of porno do not lead the adventurous sex lives that are the rule in porno; that's partially *why* they are buying the stuff—and, if the whole truth be known, that's a good part of the reason why writers and illustrators are making the stuff. The health crisis should, if anything, increase the production and consumption of porno; gays who have curtailed—or eliminated—having sex with other people still need a sexual outlet. Reading and looking at porno is just about the safest sexual action that you can do.

Pornography is a literature of the fantastic. The artist who refused to illustrate an "unsafe" story realized the story was a fantasy, but he still believed that his participation might prove harmful to the physical health of others. That sounds suspiciously like the logic the Catholic Church uses to condemn *thinking* about sex: "The Sixth Commandment forbids all impure thoughts, words, and deeds, whether alone or with others." In other words, if you think about fucking Jack Wrangler, it's the same sin—morally speaking—as actually getting it on with him. Faced with this equation of thought and action, only a cretin wouldn't say, "Oh hell, if I'm going to go to Hell anyway, I might as well go for something more than thinking." But upholders of Catholic dogma figured that if they could make you feel terrible enough about your thoughts, your deeds would take care of themselves. Now there are a growing number of people who believe that they must keep you from your "unsafe" thoughts lest you go out and commit "unsafe" acts.

Conscience and Silence

Sounds like Orwellian thought control, doesn't it? "Don't you dare *think* about swallowing cum." The artist who refused to do a drawing was saying, in effect, "I won't contribute to your 'unsafe' thoughts." The idea that drawing or writing can (or should) be so tightly controlled that it will only reflect one "acceptable" point of view would be silly if it weren't danger-ous. It is always dangerous to seek to repress expressions of thoughts—even if these thoughts are reprehensible. Still, could you imagine ever saying, "I got AIDS because of *that* drawing." (Incidentally, the artist wasn't asked to produce a drawing that in itself glorified an "unsafe" sexual practice. But he feared guilt by association, one of the weapons McCarthy found so appeal-ing and whose time has come again. In the meantime, the story itself has gone "on hold;" it may never be published. And so one person's conscience can lead to silence of another person.)

I've written—I write—a great deal of porno. While I have of my own volition curbed some of the set pieces that I used to feature (I haven't done one of those "I went to the baths last night and . . ." stories in quite a while), "unsafe" sexual practices do continue to appear in my writing. (Just as "unsafe" practices still make frequent appearances in my sexual fantasies.) But these sex acts are not happening in my life: they are occurring in pornography. Porno stories, be they as vivid and as magnificent as *Mister Benson* or *Story of O*, remain only text—not blueprints for behavior. A person who would take *Beauty's Punishment* or *The Brig* as a how-to manual had problems before he picked up the book.

Ironically, it is the pornographic magazines that have dealt most clearly with AIDS. Though the coverage of AIDS in many gay newspapers has been admirable, the reportage is frequently so technical or so political that it forgets to address the concern of the average gay man. Five hundred words on AIDS in *First Hand* or *Drummer* (often done as a prelude to "unsafe" material) does more to educate the gay community than five thousand words on the very latest AIDS research in *The Advocate* or *The Bay Area Reporter*. People connected with the production of porno tend to be very adept at getting messages across to their readers. A certain directness of style comes with the smutty territory. When this style is turned momentarily from "You'll Love Jerking Off To This" to "In Real Life, Don't Do These Things," the results can be dramatically effective. The coverage of AIDS in pornographic publications has another important aspect: gay porn magazines reach many gays who do not read non-porn gay newspapers. While many gay people who read, say, the *Advocate* also read, say, *First Hand*, many more people who read *First Hand* don't read the *Advocate*.

Porno Isn't Real Life

If porno were truly like real life, there would be no need for porno. Conventional porno is set in a universe of huge dicks, bulging muscles, superlative orgasms. (Pornography is as artificial, as constructed, as opera.) It should not be surprising that AIDS has no place in such a world. (Syphilis was never very popular on the Planet Porno, either.) It is not that pornography is unfeeling, but that pornography can feel only on its own terms. In "On Writing Pornography" (In *I Once Had A Master And Other Tales of Erotic Love*), John Preston writes of the "glee" of pornography: "I had that sense of fun while doing the writing. I felt as though I were saying to a whole group of people, 'Come and look at this one. You won't believe what I've done this time!' " All pornography is essentially joyful; it exclaims, "This is wonderful!"

The producers of gay porno don't exist in a vacuum, so AIDS has affected porno. Anonymous, promiscuous sex is being downplayed and relationship-centered sex is being promoted. But this shift isn't because pornography hates its past, but because porno is receptive to the prevailing erotic consciousness. (Some nineteenth century porno seems dumb today; the turn-ons have changed.) But porno doesn't lie; it doesn't say that something that is sexually exciting isn't. As a producer of porno, I wouldn't censure a well-written, hot scene of potentially unhealthy ass-fucking. Such a story will provide pleasure to a great many people. If providing pleasure isn't the point of all writing and drawing, what *is* the point of writing and drawing? If a lot of people don't enjoy porno, it wouldn't exist.

Pornography is essentially apolitical because sexual pleasure, which porno celebrates, is apolitical. What feels good is what feels good. What looks good is what looks good. What reads good is what reads good. Politics approaches insanity when it attempts to prove that unsafely achieved orgasms don't feel good. Politically correct gays would have us believe that awareness of the health implications of certain actions should make these actions less enjoyable. But even if we are refraining from certain actions, these actions do not lose their potential for pleasure. Sexual actions may be modified because of medical realities, but sexual feelings can't be changed. For the reader or viewer, pornography expresses exotic feelings, not sexual realities.

The Un-Christian Christian

There's no one more un-Christian than a born-again Christian, no one who's more against other people smoking cigarettes than a former four-pack-a-day man. And there's probably no one more anti-gay sex than a successful porno artist who refuses to illustrate a story because he believes the activities in the story are "unsafe." By his action, the artist joins the ranks of gays who feel it is their political duty to make other gays behave themselves. (The artist is probably suffering some guilt, too—he used to laud the very same activities he now finds verboten. And guilt is the antithesis of pornography.)

Since AIDS is a *disease*, not a political problem, the cure for AIDS will be a medical one, not a political one. AIDS is caused by a virus—not by the Everard Baths, the Mineshaft, and certainly not by pornography. Attacking porno for contributing to the number of AIDS cases betrays the fundamental lack of understanding of both porn and AIDS. AIDS has no conscience: being "good" (i.e., living a drug-free, tubs-less, porn-free life) will not prevent you from contracting AIDS; if "goodness" were the preventive vaccine for AIDS, there would be no AIDS babies. And if "badness" (being a promiscuous, porn-loving druggie) were the cause of AIDS, there would be several million PWAs by now.

In the strictest sense, pornography lacks a moral component. Porno is self-referential: it exists only in its own amoral world. As such, it's facile to maintain that "nice" people don't need the stuff, but "not-nice" people do. The "evils" of porno have been deduced through the lenses of lopsided studies. If x-number of rapists admit to liking porno, it is postulated that a link has been established between porn and rape. Some rapists probably have an affinity for Shirley Temple movies, but the point of linking porno with a social ill is not to seek to remedy the ill, but to "cure" porno. There is no causality between porn and AIDS; if one is assumed, it is to attack porn, not AIDS. Pornography bothers so many people so much that logic doesn't enter into condemnations of it.

Little Influence On Behavior

Though writers don't like to admit it, very little of what is written has much influence on readers' behavior. To maintain that a story that details the swallowing of semen will lead to readers contracting AIDS is like saying that a story that details a bodybuilder's workout will lead readers to entering the Mr.

Universe contest or that a story about sneaker fetishism will cause Nike stock to rise. Pornography can be wonderfully effective as writing, but it is never so effective that it causes readers to fundamentally alter their lifestyles. Writing and drawing can't make you do anything.

Book-burning movements always ultimately fail because, while "troublesome" books can be physically eliminated, "troublesome" ideas can't be wiped out. It would be possible, I suppose, to cleanse porno of "unsafe" sexual activities, but it would never be possible to entirely stop these practices from occurring in life and in thought. No author's works have been more often burned than those of de Sade, yet de Sade continues to exert a powerful influence on erotic writing. De Sade set up the pornographic universe, but it's fairly safe, I think, to say that if he hadn't written *The 120 Days of Sodom*, someone else would have. The pornographic imagination is simply too powerful an element in the human experience to be suppressed in literature and art.

Today's leading book-burner, Andrea Dworkin, sees porno (broadly defined and *in toto*) as causing all sorts of social ills. Her solution: eliminate the porno. (Dworkin never dwells long on the fact that people are raped and beaten and oppressed in cultures that have no access to pornography.) Some gay activists are more closely focused but their solution is equally Dworkinian: since porno influences behavior (and there is no evidence that it does), it should be purified of "unsafe" elements.

The Repression of Sexuality

Such a notion would be merely curious if publishers of gay porno weren't beginning to pay attention to it. These publishers don't believe that "unsafe" porno cause AIDS, but they are starting to think it might be easier to give in to the gays who are seeking the repression of sexuality. (No one really believes closing the baths will stop AIDS, but closing the baths is doing *something*—and many gay activists prefer action, any action, over doing nothing, even if doing nothing is the sanest action.) Few publishers of gay-oriented material have strong beliefs (other than in making money); they tend to believe whomever they talked with last. So "safe" sex porno is a hot item in porndom today. And it's pointless to argue with publishers or activists on the "safe" sex rag that *all* pornography is safe pornography.

Pornography is harmless. If porno has any lasting effect (and I'm not sure that it does, any more than any other genre has—though individual works within a genre may have), that effect is a good one. Gay porno tells us it feels great—it feels *physically* great—to be gay. That's a damn good message to hear, especially in the age of AIDS when the physical expressions of male homosexuality have come under brutal attack. To hate porno is to hate sex.

I am not arguing that all works of porno are of equal merit. But I do believe that if all pornography is to be thought of as a single "thing" (and that is the popular way to think of porno), then pornography is benevolent. Behind every great attack on porno, there is a great sexual hang-up.

Taking the Sex Out of Homosexuality

Though critics of "unsafe" gay male porno (who also tend to support closing the baths) are well-meaning, they place themselves in an impossible position by seeking to divorce homosexuality from the sexual expression of homosexuality. Since homosexuality is *defined* by sexual orientation, it is nonsense to maintain that there are sexual gays and non-sexual gays. (There are celibate gays; however, celibates aren't neuters, but people who have chosen not to give physical expression to their sexualities.) Yet when I read Randy Shilts and some gay medical writers and the pronouncements of the close-the-baths mani-acs, I can't help wondering if these people are really gay; they seem never to have had a lustful thought about another man in their lives.

There have always been gays who hated their sexuality, but the new breed of gays who preach fear and loathing of sexuality are zealously evangelical: "Y'all *don't* come, ya hear." They have found an enemy, but they are not sure whether that enemy is

AIDS or sex. Their feelings of impotence in the fight against AIDS have led them to attack sex. And when sex is attacked, pornographic works—those graphic exaltations of sex—become the faggots on the fire.

13

ZEITGEIST OR POLTERGEIST?
Why Gay Books Are So Bad

I've just read a batch of new gay books, and they're all awful. But there's no need to deconstruct these books to show why each one fails. They fail generically, as one, and they fail because of the way the publishing system for gay material is set up. Literary talent has little to do with what's published; the philosophy of the book business makes it so that dreck is about all they can publish and make a buck on.

In the last 30 years, gay literature has not managed to produce a single masterpiece. There isn't a single novel about the gay experience (except maybe Christopher Isherwood's *A Single Man* and James Baldwin's *Giovanni's Room* and, stretching things a bit, Rita Mae Brown's *Rubyfruit Jungle* and Andrew Holleran's *Dancer from the Dance*) that you'd want to share with someone outside of gay culture. There's no *Roots*, no gay *Portnoy's Complaint*, no gay *Fear of Flying*—three books that despite their flaws generated tremendous excitement; there's not even primo gay trash on the order of *Valley of the Dolls*, *I'll Take Manhattan* or *Evergreen*. While most gay books are crap, they lack the verve, the looniness, the style of the great trash masters.

The gay books I do admire are so specialized that they should carry warnings to heterosexuals: "Straights are advised that this book contains material which may not be suitable for them; gay guidance suggested." As worthwhile as *The Confessions of Danny Slocum*, the Boyd McDonald anthologies, *Restless Rednecks: Gay Tales of a Changing South, I Once Had a Master and Other Tales of Erotic Love*, and the Phil Andros books are, they require almost as much pre-knowledge as Schoenberg's *Erwartung*. Gay writers complain because they aren't reaching wide audiences, but when you read what they're writing, you understand why: just dip into *Men on Men: Best New Gay Fiction*—the majority of the selections appear to be written in a language that's almost English.

As a cultist I have a certain fondness for insular gay books, but it's disconcerting to see so many writers ignoring the bigger picture. Will there ever be a book that remains faithful to the gay experience but speaks to everyone, gay and straight alike, a gay book as passionate and popular as *Song of Solomon* or *The Chosen*? While Toni Morrison and Chaim Potok took us deeply into the lives of poor Blacks and Hasidic Jews respectively, you didn't have to be of the group each was writing about to be thrilled by these books.

The Smut and the Shame

Gay vernacular writing—not only pornography, but other genre work (mysteries, policiers, the Alex Kane series)—touches people in ways that non-genre gay books don't possibly because their writers make up in sheer skill what they may lack in literary talent. Vernacular writing constitutes the bulk of published gay material: writers are drawn to it because it's easier to get that material into print. The disproportionate amount of pornography in relation to the total volume of gay material, which has no correlation in any other minority literature, isn't entirely a matter of supply and demand. That smut sells well doesn't necessarily prove that gays are porn mavens; it does show that gays will buy the stuff they're saturated with. It's relatively easy to get a copy of *First Hand* or *Mandate* magazines, much easier than locating a copy of a gay book.

Genre writing enables writers to hone their craft. In fact, when gay writers start thinking of themselves as better than their material, when their style becomes their substance, and their adjectives their plots, they may get mainstream treatment, but they often lose their audience. (As far as reaching the most people, a gay writer can't do better than writing for the gay stroke mags.) Many gay books fail because their authors become rarified; they stop writing for the boys in the bars and they start writing for—well, that's the problem: I'm not sure who most non-genre gay books are supposed to be for. A book like the unspeakable *I've a Feeling We're Not in Kansas Anymore* probably goes over well in Fire Island Pines, thereby reaching a full one-hundredth of one percent of the gay population. What are the rest of us supposed to read?

Is it too much to ask that a gay novel tell a good story? Is storytelling politically incorrect or something? What amazed me about Paul Reed's *Facing It* and Charles Nelson's *The Boy Who Picked the Bullets Up* was not that their narratives were particularly compelling, but that they *had* narratives. The bulk of the "artier" gay material (Gluck's *Elements of a Coffee Service*, Picano's *Ambidextrous*, Ferro's *The Blue Star*, Cooper's *Safe*) may have some value as literary exercises, just as novels written without using the letter "e" would, but this curious attribute certainly doesn't make for a visceral response.

Why is gay literature in such a shameful state? Why are gay books a joke among minority literatures? Why can't you discuss gay lit in the same way as you can current Black and Jewish writing? Some clues may be found in looking at the mechanics of how and why gay books get published.

Most gay books, gay male and lesbian, fiction and non-fiction, from both mainstream and small presses, are so dreadful that when I see people buying them, I think that these books are not attracting an audience; they're inheriting one. Gay people just want to read books that touch on their experiences. They've been ripped off repeatedly, by both straight and gay publishers, yet they keep buying. Sales figures only tell that people are buying books, not that they're enjoying them. And most people don't realize how few copies of a gay book are sold: five thousand copies of a book from a major press isn't a bad sale and it's damn good by small press standards. Still, the publication of gay material is enjoying a relatively financially healthy period now (no one is making a lot of money, but enough people are making enough money to perpetuate the cycle), so there's no economic reason for publishers to want to produce better books.

Playing Safe

The mainstream plays safe. Major publishers think they are taking enough risk by simply publishing gay material. To want them to publish challenging, original gay books is asking them for the moon when they think they're already giving us the stars. Neither *Urban Aboriginals* nor *Facing It* nor *In the Life*, which, despite their problems, are three of the more interesting gay books I've read could have been published by mainstream publishers; these books took risks that major publishers wouldn't have wanted to share. It's remarkable they were published at all, but no system is foolproof.

Mainstream publishers are emulated by the small press. Publishers generally have no real love of books, but their business forces them to have contact with folks who do. Most chief honchos at publishing companies are very astute at business and so they go at books as they'd go at shirts or VCRs—"Perfecting" them, honing them to fit some poorly-defined idea of what people want, and caring next to nothing about literary values. Publishers want books they know they can sell; their critics want books that are moving experiences.

Publishers of gay material usually have terrible taste. Most of them have never read for pure pleasure. Barbara Grier of Naiad Press is the exception which proves the rule: Grier is the only publisher I can think of who has done bibliographical research on gay material. Publishers don't generally have the background, the instincts, or the information of people who have lived books, and they have no shame about not knowing anything about literature. From their point of view, such knowledge is not essential to their work: you don't need a familiarity with Gertrude Stein, Jean Genet, and Yukio Mishima to be able to understand an annual report.

The literary incompetence of publishers and more and more editors doesn't prevent them from touting themselves as creative geniuses, and they'll get very huffy if they're told that their decisions are not based in understanding literary talent, but in merely knowing how the publishing game is played. If a mainstream house wants one gay novel for its fall list because it had one such book last season that played in Peoria, there will be one such book. If it isn't a commercial failure, the editor who acquired it prides himself for knowing the market and the following season he can do another dull gay book. If a small gay press considers a hundred projects, publishes ten, and has one decent seller, the publisher will be considered a hero and will be giving interviews about the golden age of gay literature. The quality of what he publishes is of no concern to him: what's good is what sells.

Book is a Book is a Book

What sells should be what's good, but presently there's no way to test this odd, intriguing little theory. Publishers moan about having to reject good material because they say they are overwhelmed with submissions, and writers, who believe an amazing amount of the bullshit publishers dish out, say there's a need for more publishers of gay material. But new publishers would probably opt for the same sort of second-rate material that everyone's turning out. The road to literary hell is paved with the good intentions of publishers who start out saying "I'm gonna do it right; I'm not gonna screw up like Alyson or Gay Sunshine." Several projects later, these publishers are turning down the same "good material" that Alyson and Gay Sunshine did and building up the same type list they first wanted to avoid. "Don't you think I'd like to publish good books?" they ask and answer, "You know I would, but I simply cannot sell them to my readers."

That's not exactly true. The difficulties for a new publishing company aren't dependent on what kind of material it's putting out. But the publishers soon tire of difficult births and are prone to take the path of least resistance. Why bother searching out or developing topnotch material if an also-ran manuscript will sell just as well? Why bother trying to create an audience for a book or trying to reach the vast majority of gay people who have never bought a gay book? "Look at this," a publisher will say, pointing to another publisher's lousy book, "this book sold very well, and it's a quick and dirty job if ever there was one. This is what I have to compete with." Never mind that books aren't commodities you can have too many of.

Publishers are pack animals. If a publisher sells enough copies of a gay book to make some money, he'll be very receptive to another book along the same lines. Meanwhile, other publishers, quick to spot a trend, will be looking for the same knock-offs. Copy-cat publishing works against literary originality because the books that stand the best chance of being published are the ones that can be presented at editorial meetings as "just like" a recent success. The zeitgeist demands "high concept," a book that can be described in a few words. What good book could be reduced to a single catchy phrase? And the current high concepts in gay lit are rather pedestrian: a gay P.I., a married man/woman coming out, a somewhat promiscuous, recreational drug-taking, upper-middle class, white, male queer dying of AIDS/female queer dying of cancer, a teacher having a same-sex affair with a student, safe sex porn. All great books either create a genre or destroy one; in the current gay book system, there's no movement possible at all.

Story of O

If a writer, O, has an idea for a gay book, he'll either write it (which is sheer madness; the odds are overwhelmingly against the book being published no matter what its quality), or he starts talking with people at publishing houses (which can be equally mad).

Assuming O is lucky, he may actually succeed in getting past a publisher's flunkies and grab the attention of an editor who'll probably tell him, "It's an interesting idea, but we're currently working on a book like the one you're proposing." Of course, O's idea is seen as like a project the company is working on; if O's idea were too radical, he wouldn't even have gotten as far as hearing from an acquisitions editor. But most probably the book that O is proposing isn't really like the book the editor is telling him it's like. But one gay book is the same as another gay book to publishers, so if a house is committed to a new Andrew Holleran or a new Edmund White, that commitment effectively cancels out any other gay writer's chances. (Holleran's and White's diminishing capacities as writers does not affect their publishing ins: the writer the house knows is always better than the writer the house doesn't know.)

Most likely O is a terrible writer, but no one will tell him that and risk being thought crude. But if O has some talent that could be developed, he won't get any encouragement from editors or publishers. These people are too busy to devote time to writers. Ironically, a terrible writer who's tenacious may have a better chance of publication than a writer who has ability that needs nurturing. Bad writers don't need encouragement; they plow on relentlessly. But a potentially good writer who needs (and would welcome) some editorial input (and won't get it) might not continue to write; when he sees the garbage that does get published, he may think "I can never do that" and give up entirely.

Should O go to a small gay publisher with an idea for a book, he'll probably be told, "Sure, send it to us when you're done." And when he finishes the book, he'll hear, "This doesn't do anything for me." This rules out O's book—and O. The publisher doesn't care if O has a writing talent worth developing because right now the publisher is, say, too wrapped up trying to sell X's book, which may be stinko (and everyone knows it), but. . . . And here the possible permutations are endless (God alone knows all the kinds of deals that are struck to get gay books into print, but the whole business gets very incestuous; the same names keep popping up all over the place so you could think of gay publishing as a never-ending game of "Round Up the Usual Suspects")—X is an editor at a major house who might be good for a big reprint sale some day, X's book is in a boring, safe formula, X is fucking someone—well— at the publishing house, X's book is rank porn, which is always easy to break even on. You have to be incredibly stupid to go broke publishing pornography.

Maxims of Misinformation

Publishing houses have their sacred groups of misconceptions, and they simply ignore any opinions contrary to the official line of thought. "Collections don't sell" is one such holy maxim (except, of course, when, like the Boyd McDonald sex writing anthologies, they do). Another is "People don't want to read about _____." Fill in the blank: SM, politics, New York, writers, Vietnam, lesbian nuns—oops, scratch the last one. But often the best books are about subjects people don't want to read about; good writing will always draw people to its subject. Essentially, all bits of falsely-reasoned publishing scripture boil down to "We don't know how to sell it and we're not gonna try" or—as this law is more commonly expressed—"There's no market for it." That's the final word, and there's no sense arguing that a good book could create its own market.

Since all publishers play by the same rules, writers easily become demoralized. Writers are seen by editors and publishers as their enemies. The less secure the editor or publisher is, the more frequently he says no. The publishing business treats all but a very few top writers, those who have consistently produced big money-makers, with indifference or contempt. Publishers and editors would probably like to find a way to produce books without using writers. Maxwell Perkins is dead, and we will never see his kind again.

More Problems

If a writer does get a contract for a gay book, his problems are just beginning. There will likely be endless fights about revisions. The publisher may decide, for example, that sex is out or that sex is in and demand that all books conform to this dictum. Publishers aren't going to give the book much promotion, so when the book doesn't do spectacularly well, they'll be able to question the validity of the gay book market. And publishers can also blame the critics, particularly at the New York *Times*, for a gay book's disappointing sales. (Gay reviewers who don't praise everything queer that comes off the presses are considered "traitors"; though a publisher's pet, like Ethan Mordden, will get to periodically attack other gay writers in the *Advocate*.) Of the several hundred books produced each year that have a strong appeal to the gay market, only a handful get reviewed by the *Times*. To get a *Times* review, a gay book generally must be by a well-known writer preferably not performing at his best, or be so ferociously learned, like John Boswell's *Christianity, Social Tolerance, and Homosexuality*, that the *Times* would lose intellectual credibility by not noticing it. (The *Times* did, however, get away with a brief snide review of Richard Plante's *The Pink Triangle*, surely the major gay book of 1986.) But the *Times*, with its long homophobic history, isn't the likeliest place to look for support for gay books anyway, so it's not strange not to see many gay books reviewed or advertised there. What is strange is not seeing more gay books advertised in the gay press. Ads in a typical issue of *The New York Native*, for example, would have us believing that Alyson Publications is the only company producing gay books.

The gay small presses seem determined to remain insignificant. Though they don't have the resources big time houses do, they often seem to be hiding behind the selfserving idea that they are doomed not to sell many copies of their books no matter what they do. There's no textural reason why Gay Sunshine's *Facing It* shouldn't have been a phenomenal best-seller (by small press standards, that's 25,000 copies; *Facing It* sold about a fifth of that), but the book was almost cruelly mis-promoted, as if the publisher didn't have the confidence that any publisher should have in any book he produces. The small presses lack the determination to break out of their ghettos; they don't often use all the business opportunities open to them, and if they try to show savvy, they get jumped on by activists who think success means selling out. Barbara Grier was crucified for her promotion of *Lesbian Nuns*, but she was just doing what any publisher should do with good hot property.

The absence of political will on the part of gay small presses might be understood if they resisted success out of a desire to devote themselves to books that were particularly demanding of readers and, as such, wouldn't be able to find a large audience. But almost all of what the gay small presses produce is simplistic material for very general gay audiences. Yet gay publishers promote these books as if they were selling the homosexual equivalent of *Finnegan's Wake*; what they are selling is typically a fag/dyke Harlequin romance.

There's a thin line in the gay small presses that separates a failure from a success, often just a couple of hundred copies. You'd think small presses would be willing to take chances, but these houses are often just as stodgy as the most conservative mainstream publishers. Gay publishers don't bother developing good projects since the very worst that a bad project can do is "fail"—which will be offset by a bad project that "succeeds."

Wasted Time, Wasted Trees

What isn't generally understood is how much talent and hard work are wasted; if it were all channeled productively, something resembling a gay literature might result. As it is now, perfectly publishable manuscripts (which, while not all masterpieces, are at least no worse than most of what is published) can bounce around publishing houses for years until the writers no longer remember why they wrote the books in the first place and are too disgusted to continue peddling the scripts. There isn't a gay writer who doesn't have a personal collection of horror stories with publishers and editors cast as Dracula and his son, all variations on the theme of writers feeling victimized by the publishing system. They feel victimized because they don't understand how the system works. In essence: if an editor goes along with another tired book on an overdone idea and the book fails, it won't be his fault, but if he pushes a quirky, interesting new idea that fails, he's thought to have lost his touch. The key to getting published is giving publishers and editors what they want, but what they want isn't—can't be— good because they don't bring literary standards to their judgments.

Basically, a superlative gay manuscript is a manuscript that St. Martin's Press or NAL has accepted. A good gay manuscript is a manuscript that Alyson or Naiad has accepted. A bad gay manuscript is a manuscript that St. Martin's, NAL, Alyson, and Naiad have turned down. The decision making involved is highly capricious. (Who you know doesn't hurt.) In the universe of publishing realpolitik, it's not just that the decisions about what gets published might have been made by anyone, but that the books which result frequently read like they could have been written by anyone.

My Brother, My Lover is a particularly atrocious recent gay novel, a tragic accident that no one tried to prevent. Didn't anyone connected with this book realize what rotten stuff they were working on? Or is there a deep cynicism here, an attempt to show that gay people will read anything, that it doesn't matter what a publisher produces because the audience has no class, no discernment, no critical facilities?

Publishers don't see writers as individual. So even if a writer has a moderately successful gay book for a publisher, that's no guarantee that the publisher will be at all interested in what the writer does next. The publisher will likely have a "first refusal" contract with the writer, but by the time the writer completes a second book, the publisher will have forgotten about the writer because in the publisher's mind the writer is interchangeable with any number of other gay writers. With such an attitude on the publishers' parts, it's no wonder that not only are so many gay books bad, but they're bad in the same way—unsure, hesitant, depersonalized, artless, mindless. After I've read a half-dozen or so bad gay books they tend to blend together in my mind; it's difficult to believe each was written by a different person.

When writers are perceived as being without personalities when publishers think, "If he won't do it my way, someone else will," publishing loses its soul. Publishing has always been a business first, but only fairly recently has publishing become a business like any other business. Gay writers, I think, almost all feel privileged to be able to write about the gay experience. (If they don't, there's always a publisher to tell them, "If it weren't for me, you'd have no hope of getting published at all.") Gay writers aren't fools, but they are certainly not writing principally for the money. If a writer realizes $1,500 or $2,000 from a gay small press book (and often not very much more than that from a mainstream production), a book which may have taken him a year or more to write—almost no gay writer can afford to write full time—he's doing good. But he'll probably not be in a hurry to work on another book. The hassles aren't worth it.

Bad books drive out good. Gay books are so bad because the publishing system demands that many of them be reductions of the gay experience to the most common denominators. At one time, any book about homosexuality was revolutionary no matter what its literary merit. Today, for the most part, gay books are updates of *The Homosexual in America* and *The Well of Loneliness.* If something is worth doing, the publishing wisdom holds, it is worth doing over and over and over again until no one remembers why there was ever any interest in the subject in the first place. The real losers are the readers, caught between the rock of unadventurous publishers and the hard place of mediocre writers.

14

YOU OUGHT TO BE
IN WORDS

I know what quite a few of you are thinking: "I've always wanted to be a writer. I know I could write better than most of the people in this publication." But remember: as the noted philosopher, Fran Lebowitz, has remarked, "In the land of the blind the one-eyed man is a writer and he's not too thrilled about it."

Still, no matter who says what, there are those of you out there who harbor deep in the darkest recesses of your consciousness—right next to your disgusting fantasies about Christopher Atkins—the wish to write. No amount of excessively rational discourse on my part will persuade you to abandon this perverted desire.

No doubt many of you budding writers are drawn to the craft (and writing is *not* an art, like being a sculptor; it's a craft, like being a Roto-Rooter person) because you believe it is the road to incredible riches, great fame, and fabulous tricks. Sit down, I have bad news for you. Bad news about money: The IRS cried over my last tax return and asked me if they could do anything to help me out financially. Bad news about notoriety: close your eyes and try to remember the name of the writer of this essay. Bad news about sex: you don't want to know, but whenever I tell someone I'm a writer, he immediately wants to know if I have Mister Benson's phone number.

Writing is indeed a sordid profession, but somebody's got to do it. It's like being a Topman. But being a writer is also *unlike* being a Topman because writing is something you can fake by simply mastering (or slaving?) a few simple suggestions (or if you are truly serious about writing, consider them The Ten Commandments), which I will thoughtfully list.

1. If you don't already have at least four or five, develop harmful habits. The tried and true—smoking, drinking, drugging, gambling, relentless promiscuity—may work in a pinch (and a good writer always keeps these habits on tap in case of an emergency), but really creative writers prefer more inventive, but equally potentially lethal pastimes such as watching *Dallas* with a sincere interest in Sue Ellen Ewing, preparing and eating the recipes printed in women's magazines, saying good things about Eddie Murphy while in the company of the politically correct, *being* politically correct, and talking to editors about money.

2. Get an agent. Every writer needs an agent. It just make sense: the aggravation an agent produces will keep you thin. God and publishers hate fat writers.

3. Become an expert in some very esoteric area which you will then try to write about at undue length. Notice: wine enemas, underwater cocksucking, and trying to be amusing about the rather ugly subject of writing are already taken.

4. Have friends who are writers. Remember a truly great writer is known by how much he *doesn't* write. Would J.D. Salinger be a household word today if he endlessly churned out articles for gay magazines? Not hardly. And the best way to artistically "not write" is to number among your acquaintances many other truly great writers. You will pave the way to your and others' success by having long telephone conversations with these other writers, conversations mainly about who is not writing the most.

5. Develop your neuroses. No one can really call himself a writer unless he is severely paranoid, hopelessly hypochondriacal, and/or possessed of a dreadful phobia or seventeen. However those writers aiming for the Nobel and/or Pulitzer Prizes would be wise to consider developing entirely *new*

neuroses, such as Stickiophobia—the morbid fear of scotch tape, Editorial Dementia Praecox—the irrational belief that publishers always tell the truth, or Oopsaphrenia—the inability to understand the meaning of the word "deadline."

6. Reduce your vocabulary to a few choice phrases, judicious use of which will provide the answer to every possible question that may be asked you by editors and other unsavory characters you will come in contact with in your new role as a writer: "Don't blame me, blame the fuckin' Post Office," "Next week, I promise," "My agent handles that," "No," "That's my other line—goodbye."

7. Sleep correctly. Some people are most productive during daylight hours and sleep at nighttime. Others work best at night and sleep during the day. If you want to be a writer you need to revise your schedule so that you are sleeping when you should be working. As a most illuminating illustration: Since I am most inclined to write during the morning hours, I make it a point never to awaken before two in the afternoon.

8. Cultivate your prejudices. Yes, yes, yes, it's all well and good to denounce prejudice of every variety. But you wouldn't want to be a writer if you were well and good, would you now? Does Rita Mae Brown write about how wonderful men are? Have you ever read a bad word about S/M in *Drummer*? Would Daniel Curzon write "Homage To Twinkies"? Can you conceive of Andrew Holleran telling all about why Fire Island is a terrible place? Would John Preston write promo for Izod Lacostes? Of course not. And you, too, have your prejudices: *exploit them!* I myself never have anything good to write about people who aren't into their tits, clean jockstraps, and Republicans. Nor would I ever write ill of piss scenes, Bette Davis, and big dicks relentlessly fucking my tight, quivering rectum.

9. Invent a mother. All writers seem to be cursed by real mothers who are (or were—may they rest in peace) exceptionally loving, pleasant, and kind. Writing about such mothers doesn't sell. On the other hand, hysterically eccentric mothers, cold, cruel mothers, and cigar-smoking lesbian mothers are the stuff that best sellers are made of. I'm sorry: that's the way it is. You don't find me complaining just because my own loving,

pleasant, kind mother disowned me after she read my story about her called "The Castrating Zionist."

10. As an extreme measure, die. Everyone loves dead writers because they're not always kvetching about something-or-other.